FROM
SEA TO SKY

Dr Sneha Verghese is a double postgraduate in Biotechnology and Journalism, and holds a PhD in Mass Communication and Journalism. She works for the Indian Council of Agricultural Research, but her passion is writing. While science writing is her forte, she has been a freelance writer and columnist for various newspapers and magazines, and her literary work has appeared in well-acclaimed anthologies. Sneha lives in Hyderabad.

FROM SEA TO SKY

Hidden Stories of Nature's Science

SNEHA VERGHESE

Illustrations by Ishan Trivedi

hachette INDIA

First published in paperback in 2025 by Hachette India
(Registered name: Hachette Book Publishing India Pvt. Ltd)
An Hachette UK company
www.hachetteindia.com

1

Versions of the essays in this book first appeared in the *Young Hans* supplement of *The Hans India* in the column 'Nature Narratives' between 2015 and 2018, and are included with the permission of the newspaper.

Illustrations by Ishan Trivedi
Diagrams on Page 36 by Syed Salahuddin
Story title and margin design elements from freepik.com free downloads

ISBN 978-93-5731-399-5

Hachette Book Publishing India Pvt. Ltd
4th & 5th Floors, Corporate Centre
Plot No. 94, Sector 44, Gurugram – 122003, India

Typeset by Manmohan Kumar, Delhi

Printed and bound in India
by Thomson Press India Ltd.

FSC www.fsc.org
MIX
Paper | Supporting responsible forestry
FSC® C010615

To
my mother

For believing in me enough
to make my dreams come true.
For standing by me all through her battles,
and mine too.

CONTENTS

1

THE CLOWNFISH'S BODYGUARD

Mr Serene, the gigantic old sea turtle, was waddling along the ocean floor off the sea coast of Australia when he heard a tiny voice in his ear.

'Excuse me, Sir, I am Funny...you know...a clownfish. And I was...uh...wondering if...huh...'

Mr Serene turned his head to look at where the voice was coming from. Mr Serene was very, very old, and his eyesight wasn't very good. He blinked a few times and peered hard at the fish in front of him. It was small in size, but its orange and white colouring made it look gorgeous.

'I can see that you're a clownfish, but you're not funny at all,' said the turtle in a bored voice.

'Oh no – no, sir, I didn't mean that...' stammered the poor clownfish, now red with embarrassment. 'You see, "Funny" is my name...that's what I'm called.

I'm new to this part of the ocean, and I would like to know if there is any suitable place which I could make my home.'

'Well, there are corals here...and you could always stay under those big rocks that lie scattered around,' said Mr Serene slowly.

'What about those different coloured flowers with long petals, sir?' queried Funny, pointing towards brightly coloured flower-like structures attached to rocks, spread all over the ocean floor. 'Can I stay there, or is someone already staying there?'

The turtle became grave. 'No fish goes near them, clownfish!' he warned. 'Those are sea anemones – strange, deadly creatures – half-plant and half-animal. Those things that you call petals are horrible tentacles that sting and poison its prey, and with those same tentacles, the sea anemone pushes down its victim into its mouth at the base of the tentacles! Stay away from them if you value your life.'

Funny the clownfish shuddered at this piece of information. To think that he had considered such a monstrous creature to be his beautiful home! How fortunate for him that the turtle had warned him in time! Funny sighed. Now he would have to search for a new home.

He wished he hadn't strayed away from his old home at all. The strong currents had brought him to this strange, new, terrifying place. He felt that there were predators lurking in the dark shadows, watching him and waiting for a chance to pounce on him. He tried to keep close to the rocks to avoid being seen. He hadn't gone far when he heard a voice behind him.

'Going somewhere, Mr Clownfish?'

It was a shark! Funny didn't even bother to answer. He just darted away as fast as he could! The shark was right behind him in hot pursuit.

'Stop right there, you clownfish! You're my snack for today!' Funny heard the shark hollering behind him. He swam faster, trying to avoid the swarms of salmon and schools of dolphins on the way.

Soon, Funny felt his energy draining. The shark was gaining on him. Funny spotted more sharks coming his way from other directions. As a last resort, Funny made a dive, his eyes tightly shut. He was shooting down to the ocean floor at top speed. The shark was still chasing him. He opened his eyes, hoping he would find a hole or a rock crevice at the bottom that he could escape into. Instead, he found himself hurtling straight towards...a huge sea anemone.

It was too late to change course. Funny felt that he would meet his death one way or the other – either between the shark's jaws or in the tentacles of the anemone. He fell into the sea anemone. The shark, which had been bent upon eating Funny, swam away in a hurry when he saw the long, frightening limbs of the sea anemone. He didn't want to be stung.

Funny lay there, shivering, waiting for the tentacles to sting him and the anemone to devour him.

But nothing happened. He felt the tentacles all around him, brushing against his body pleasantly, but no stinging sensation. Funny wondered what kind of miracle this was. He looked around and, to his surprise, found another clownfish staring at him through the tentacles of the anemone. 'What's happening?' he asked the other clownfish. 'I heard this anemone can sting and kill fish. But it hasn't!'

'It can't sting us, because we have a very thick slimy layer on our bodies protecting us – other fish don't have such a fat layer,' replied the other clownfish. 'In fact, this is my home,' he continued. 'This sea anemone acts as my bodyguard, keeping me safe from all the bigger fish in this ocean as they fear the anemone. The anemone is also happy to let me stay here as it can eat the bits of food that I drop. When bigger unsuspecting fish chase me, I lead them here and they themselves become food for the sea anemone.'

Funny was thrilled. Now he didn't need to be scared anymore. 'That means I can make an anemone my home?' he cried. 'Hurray!'

'If you don't mind sharing a home, you're welcome to stay here,' said the other clownfish, smiling.

What more could Funny want? He happily agreed!

Do clownfish live with sea anemones?

Yes, they do!

Sea anemones are water-dwelling, carnivorous animals, but are 'sedentary' plants: they can't move about. They have traits of both plants and animals. They are found on ocean floors, attached to rocks by a 'foot' or a base, with many brightly coloured tentacles surrounding a central mouth. The tentacles are highly sensitive and react to the slightest touch. They have to wait for their food to swim by. When a prey comes very close, the tentacles grasp it, sting a deadly poison into it to paralyse the victim, and then push the food towards its mouth. The prey is then swallowed and digested.

The clownfish forms a 'symbiotic' relationship with the sea anemone, which means it's a partnership that benefits both. The sea anemone does not harm the clownfish because of the thick mucus layer on its body, and so the clownfish shelters in it. In return, the clownfish helps the anemone by keeping it clean (by eating the algae growing nearby or by feeding on the leftover food particles in the reef), attracting prey, and dropping scraps of its own food, which are later eaten by the anemone.

Different kinds of sea anemone

2

THE EMU'S YOGA CLASS

'Never in my life did I think I could be affected so – it's a tragedy,' Martha the garden snail said, wiping her eyes on a blade of grass. Her neighbour, Tracey the squirrel, was listening to her tale of woe and nodding her head in sympathy at every pause.

'Don't be so sad, Martha, we are all in the same boat, I tell you,' said Tracey, trying to console the woebegone snail. Martha was facing a huge problem – she had become forgetful, and it was bothering her tremendously. She had never forgotten anything before. The pigeon, who was her doctor, said that she was under stress.

And why wouldn't she be? The garden where she lived had become more and more crowded with snails. Her worry was that she wouldn't be able to find enough food for herself with so many snails around. It was so bad that she couldn't even remember what she had done a few minutes earlier.

'I forget lots of things myself,' continued the squirrel, 'I work hard all through the summer, collect all the nuts I can find and bury them in the ground, hoping I can eat them during the winter months when food is scarce. And what happens? I forget where I buried them!'

'Yes, but you were always forgetful,' said Martha. 'In fact, your entire family was forgetful. Your mother and her mother, and your mother's grandmother before that. The whole lot of them used to forget where they hid their winter stash. But my family? Never did we forget a single thing !'

Tracey was quite annoyed. Why drag her family into this? Martha didn't have to defame her entire family for their poor memory! But she maintained a dignified silence.

'Well, you needn't create such a scene about it,' said Tracey dryly. 'My friend, Jason the blue jay, who lives in Florida, has the same problem. He can't find his winter supplies either, due to his forgetfulness. And he is such a smart bird otherwise! But we can't help it, you know. It happens. We can't do anything to get a good memory now.'

Just then, a voice interrupted them. 'What if you *can* get good memory power even now?'

Tracey and Martha turned around. It was a red fox. Now, red foxes had a poor reputation in Australia, where this entire conversation was taking place. Red foxes were outsiders, who had been brought to Australia by humans from Great Britain, and ever since then, the foxes had only wreaked havoc in the continent.

'I think I can help you,' said the red fox, whose name was Red too. 'I have a friend, Sharon, the emu who conducts a yoga class for all animals, especially the ones with poor memory. Haven't you heard? Yoga helps reduce stress, and improves concentration and memory power!'

Now, Tracey was wary of the fox and did not trust him at all. But Martha was desperate. 'Please, let's go to that class,' she begged Tracey. 'I'll do anything to get my memory power back.'

After some thought, Tracey agreed. She wrote to her friend Jason as well, and the blue jay joined them too. Red Fox said he was Sharon's agent and took a good part of their food stores as fees for the class. The three were joined by a goldfish, who said he was quite confident about his own memory but was always called a silly absent-minded creature by all other animals. Red Fox had convinced him too that Sharon's yoga class was the best solution.

It was a day's journey to Sharon's home. The emu was a flightless bird, about two metres tall, and the largest bird in Australia. Its keen eyes and its ability to run extremely fast captivated them, and Martha was convinced that if anyone could solve her problem, it was Sharon. The emu's sheer size was another convincing factor, as she was nothing like the puny little pigeons that Martha was used to seeing back home. Red Fox spoke to Sharon first in private, and then the emu met them.

'Nice of you all to come,' Sharon said cheerfully. 'Mr Fox has told me everything. Don't worry. We can solve all your problems. Settle in today, and we shall start the classes tomorrow.'

***

The next day, Martha, Tracey, Jason and the goldfish were up early for the yoga class. They came across Sharon pecking at some plants and shiny objects on the ground.

'So shall we start?' Martha asked eagerly.

'Start what?' said the emu absent-mindedly.

'The yoga class, of course!' said Jason.

Sharon gave them all a puzzled look. 'I don't know who you are...don't know what you all are talking about,' she muttered, and moved away to poke at some new plant.

The 'students' looked at each other in shock.

Someone cackled loudly behind them. 'So that fox fooled you too!' It was a parrot.

'What do you mean?' said Tracey angrily. 'We paid for the yoga class and we've been cheated! We won't let this emu go scot-free.'

'Leave the poor emu alone,' said the parrot. 'It doesn't know a thing. The emu is a very forgetful creature – every day is a new day for it. Red Fox knows this, and he takes advantage of poor Sharon as well as other animals like you. Go home now.'

The four animals were very upset. 'Now what do I do?' cried Martha. 'How will I improve my memory?'

But what *could* they do? The fox had already given them the slip!

Do animals forget?

Yes, they do!

Emus are large, flightless birds in Australia, and have a very short memory span. They forget an incident as soon as it's over! We know this because emus cannot recognize their trainer, no matter how many times they have seen them. And because of their poor memory power, it is very, very hard to teach them tricks that other animals learn easily. They may be great runners (with speeds of 40–48 kmph) but, unfortunately, aren't very good at remembering stuff. It doesn't make much difference to them, as they have very few predators because of their huge size and running speed.

In the same way, animals such as squirrels and blue jays always hide food to last them through winter, and both forget where they hid them! They can find only 20 per cent of what they hide. Goldfish were earlier considered to have a memory span of just 3 seconds, but recent studies show that they can record memories much longer than that. Usually, snails have average memory power. Snails have much fewer neurons compared to humans, but these neurons are also larger in size, letting us study their activity. Experiments with snails have shown that they can be trained to behave in specific ways, and this gets recorded in its neurons. But when they are under stress, for example, when there is overcrowding or pollution in their habitat, they simply cannot remember, because the neuron activity changes visibly and they fail to behave as trained earlier.

On the other hand, there are several creatures with excellent memory power, like elephants, crows, dolphins and chimpanzees.

Studies vary, but the following animals are generally known to have the best memory power!

1. ELEPHANTS
2. DOLPHINS
3. CHIMPANZEES
4. CROWS
5. DOGS
6. OCTOPUSES
7. PARROTS
8. RATS
9. PIGEONS
10. SQUIRRELS

3

CAN'T DO WITHOUT MR LAZY

The Amazon rainforest in South America was always a busy place, teeming with activity. All the animals were hard-working creatures, and they prided themselves on it. They knew that they played important roles in keeping the forest healthy and thriving, and took their responsibility very seriously indeed!

The animals often had regular meetings to discuss their problems and voice their complaints or suggestions. Carlos, the spider monkey, was getting ready to go to the meeting. He smoothened his coat with his long fingers, and carefully picked out the leaves and twigs stuck in his fur. He was just attempting to remove a few lice too, when his wife started laughing at him. 'Don't bother taking out the lice – you have far too many!' she said, giggling. 'Just take care not to scratch in front of the others.'

Carlos was annoyed. 'As if you don't have any lice on you,' he grumbled, but stopped his grooming immediately and set out. He swung from tree to tree happily, waving and talking to other animals who were on their way too. 'Yes, Uncle Macaw, I am participating in the Scratch and Win Bananas contest and I shall—'

BUMP!

Carlos had collided straight into another animal on the tree as he was busy answering the macaw. Carlos immediately murmured an apology, expecting an angry outburst. But nothing like that happened, so Carlos looked up to see who it was.

Hanging upside down from the tree was an animal the size of a dog. It had long arms and legs, a flat head and a sleepy face. It had long, strong claws, which it used to get a stronghold on the branch it was hanging from. Its greenish-grey fur had grown in an upside-down way and pointed in different directions haphazardly, unlike Carlos's smooth fur which all stood up in the same direction. Carlos felt it was an awfully smelly creature. It looked as if it had been sleeping and didn't seem in the least bothered by Carlos.

Carlos realized that this was the animal called the 'sloth'. He had often heard about them being lazy creatures but had never expected them to sleep during broad daylight. 'Uh...aren't you coming to the meeting?' he asked. The sloth slowly opened his sleepy eyes and gave a very, very, slow grin. But he didn't speak.

'Um...I think you should come,' continued Carlos, 'I suppose you have attended the meetings before?'

The sloth very slowly shook his head from side to side. Carlos took that as a 'No'.

'Well then, come with me now,' said Carlos, thinking of taking the sloth along with him. The sloth did not seem to hear him, for he closed his eyes and went back to sleep, just as he was.

Carlos felt indignant. Here he was, trying to make the sloth a responsible citizen of the jungle, and it was squarely ignoring him! He muttered under his breath.

The macaw called to him again. 'Forget him,' he said, 'he's always been a lazy bag of bones. Let's go.'

***

Carlos left the sloth hanging there and went with the macaw. 'His name is Mr Lazy,' said the macaw, as they went along. 'Being a sloth, he never ever comes down from the tree. He sleeps 20 hours of the day.'

Carlos was astonished. 'Then what does he eat?' he asked. 'And what about meeting others of his kind?'

'Oh, he eats the leaves and twigs of the tree he lives on. And none of his kind really bothers to meet others. The only way a sloth will ever see another is if there are two of them hanging on the same tree. I tell you, they are extremely sluggish!'

Carlos was quite unhappy about this. Here were animals like himself, working hard, moving around, finding food, and following the ways of the jungle in one way or the other. On the other hand, there were these sloths, who didn't even budge from their place! It was so unfair! Why did they have to share the jungle with those useless sloths?

All through the meeting, he sat in a daze, thinking about the sloths. The more he thought about them, the angrier he got. He felt they didn't deserve a place in the jungle. As the meeting came to a close, he got up.

'Friends, I have a very serious complaint to make,' Carlos announced in a grave voice, 'It's about the sloths.' A wave of surprise swept over the audience. 'These sloths live in our forest but do nothing at all. They are slow to move, always asleep and the laziest of all the animals I have ever seen. I propose that we get rid of these useless animals immediately!'

The gathering collapsed into silence. At first, it seemed downright mean to be so hostile towards another animal. But as they thought over the monkey's words, they began to agree with him.

The jaguar, who was the sloth's natural enemy, licked his lips at the prospect. If all the jungle animals decided to get rid of the sloths, he could eat them to his heart's content! He was the first to speak up in support of Carlos. 'Yes, those lazy creatures don't deserve any mercy,' he said, and turned to the other animals. 'What Carlos says is right! Let's go after the sloths!' His words injected fresh fury into the hearts of the hard-working animals, and they all shouted in unison, 'Down with the sloths!'

The maddened crowd, led by Carlos, made their way to the tree where Mr Lazy was still asleep. Mr Lazy, hearing the commotion, woke up and saw the angry faces of all the jungle animals. Surprised, he let go of his hold on the branch and fell to the ground below. He took quite a while trying to get up and shift himself to a sitting position.

'There he is!' cried Carlos. 'You can all see how slow and lethargic he is. We don't need sloths here! Get him!'

Mr Lazy realized what all the commotion was about. He felt his heart break with grief – all his life, neither had he ever hurt anyone nor troubled any creature.

How could everyone turn against him? A large tear rolled out of his eye.

The jaguar bounded forward, his mouth watering, his jaws itching to bite into his meal. The sloth sat there, as if paralyzed.

Just then a hundred tiny voices screamed out of nowhere:

'STOP! Don't you dare touch Mr Lazy!'

The jaguar stopped in its tracks, startled.

The voices seemed to be coming from Mr Lazy himself! And, suddenly, out of Mr Lazy's fur came a swarm of beetles, a battalion of cockroaches and a flurry of moths.

'We will not allow you to hurt Mr Lazy,' a beetle said. 'He has given not only us but many more tiny creatures a home to live in.'

'Why do you think his fur looks green? It's because of the algae that live on it,' said a moth.

'You think he is useless, do you?' said a cockroach. 'Let me tell you, there is a small world living right here on his body. If you kill Mr Lazy, you're killing all of us too!'

All the animals stood rooted to their spot, shocked out of their wits. Carlos was too ashamed to speak. How could he have judged the sloth so wrongly? The animals, one by one, apologized to Mr Lazy and went back to their homes, leaving the sloth in peace.

Only the jaguar went back disappointed. He felt cheated of a feast!

Are the sloths really so slow?

Yes, they are!

Sloths are tree-dwelling mammals that look very much like monkeys, but are extremely lethargic and slow. With a four-part stomach, a very slow digestive system, and a diet which mainly consists of leaves and buds, it is no surprise that they do not get enough energy to move around actively. They sleep for up to 20 hours a day, and come down from the trees only to pee and poop (and they poop only once a week!)! That's why lazy people are called 'slothful'. Because sloths hardly move around, their fur is home to several species of moths, beetles, cockroaches, unicellular organisms called ciliates, algae and fungi – in fact, a small ecosystem (a community of living and non-living things) exists right on its body!

The greenish colouration given by the algae helps the sloth blend into its forest surroundings, keeping it safe from predators. Its long, sharp claws are its only defence, and these claws are more of a hindrance to movement when on land. But, surprise, surprise – sloths are very fast swimmers.

4

PRAYING FOR PREY

'No...no...I don't like this,' Horace the garden lizard almost convulsed in horror. 'You've eaten how many leaves of the zinnia plants, you say? Fifty-five? *Fifty*-five??' He recovered, gulped a few times, and said, 'No. Not possible.'

'Oh, come on, those are just leaves,' said the butterfly. 'I am not eating up flowers, am I? Nobody's even going to notice a few missing leaves in this huge garden.'

'I won't notice one, I can understand two and I may forgive three. But fifty-five at one go? If you ate that many then, who knows how much you may eat up now? Old habits die hard.' Horace sounded firm, his face set.

'But that was when I was a kid,' moaned the butterfly. 'Just a little caterpillar! Why can't you let me in now?'

'Never. Eating up fifty-five leaves and spoiling the garden is just criminal,' said Horace. 'No, you cannot enter.' And that was that.

The butterfly flew away, muttering under her breath. She had hoped to find a healthy zinnia plant to lay her eggs.

***

Horace smiled to himself in satisfaction. Nobody, not even the tiniest creature, was allowed into his garden without his permission, and he interviewed every creature who sought admission inside. He called himself the Garden Guardian, the one who stood watch over the beautiful garden that belonged to a landlord. And funnily, all creatures obeyed him and waited for his permission to enter. Even the neighbourhood cat slunk away, scared, seeing Horace's bulging eyes, blood-red throat and menacing attitude.

Horace was, of course, quite proud of his position. He had assumed the responsibility when once, by chance, the garden had fallen to ruin, with the well drying up and the plants dying, and several of the plants infested and eaten up by insects.

Every other creature left the place one by one. Only Horace stayed back, and one day, when the rains burst forth unexpectedly, the garden also burst into bloom. And that day, Horace assumed the guardianship of the place, vowing to keep it blossoming always, and careful about whom he let into his garden.

He was quite possessive about who ate what, and how much of it. He controlled the number of plant-eating insects he let inside, because they could destroy all the plants. He wouldn't allow many carnivorous creatures in either, because they could be aggressive and would not listen to him. So he kept the garden population to a minimum. So, for a very, very long time, the garden was entirely in Horace's control.

It wasn't a great experience for the creatures that had got admission into the garden either. They didn't like being under the Garden Guardian's thumb all the time and often complained to each other in whispers about it. They hoped that someday Horace would stop being so high-handed.

Then one day, the inevitable happened. Two plant-fleas stole in and happily set up a home among the plants, escaping notice. But their babies grew and began to multiply. Then the babies' babies grew up and then they multiplied as well! Very soon, all the plants were infested with fleas.

This annoyed Horace to no end. He went around trying to eat up the fleas on his own. But there were too many!

And, unfortunately for Horace, while he was trying to eat the fleas in the west side of the garden, a few grasshoppers came in by the east wall! And while he tried to drive the grasshoppers away, some spiders managed to build their cobwebs among the bigger leaves! It was total mayhem, and now all the creatures outside the garden knew that this was a good time to try and get in, because Horace couldn't manage being both the flea-controller *and* the Garden Guardian.

After several unsuccessful attempts at solving the problem, Horace confided in an earthworm. 'I need an assistant,' said Horace, a little sadly. 'I am getting old, and these fleas will be the death of me. My beautiful garden will end up in ruin again!'

The earthworm thought for a while. 'I'll spread the word,' he said, 'but what kind of assistant are you looking for?'

'Someone who is calm and composed, who doesn't lose his cool like me when the going gets tough,' said the lizard. 'Someone who is a nice guy, not the type who'll create trouble.'

The earthworm promised to do his best. Word spread, but no one wanted to be Horace's assistant. The main reason was that they thought Horace had been selfish all this time and didn't deserve help. Horace was in despair. His garden was going from bad to worse.

***

Then, one day, there turned up in front of him an insect he had never seen before. It was quite large, green all over, and had long legs. Its forelegs were, in fact, broad and folded together as if in prayer. Horace stared at it in wonder.

'That's a praying mantis,' whispered the earthworm to Horace.

'You mean he's religious?' Horace whispered back.

'Well, it definitely does look like it,' said the earthworm.

Horace started asking the newcomer questions.

'Can you get rid of the fleas?

'Can you take care of the garden when I am not there?

'What about your diet? What do you eat? Will you eat the plants?'

The praying mantis stood silently. He didn't answer at all.

'Is he dumb?' whispered Horace.

'Maybe it's a part of his spiritual ways,' the earthworm said in a low tone.

'He didn't even say anything about what he eats,' hissed Horace.

'Maybe he fasts too,' the earthworm hissed back.

Horace was happy. Here was a perfect assistant! Someone who didn't seem to eat nor talk, and who seemed to be praying all the time. He just hoped the mantis could keep intruders out of the garden.

The following days were a dream for Horace. The mantis seemed to be very efficient at keeping out trespassers. Strangely, even some of the existing residents of the garden seemed to be disappearing.

However, Horace himself never saw the mantis move from his position. He seemed to always sit still in his praying position. Every time Horace thought of asking the mantis, he reminded himself, 'He's praying; I shouldn't disturb him.'

Very soon, the garden was under control. In fact, there wasn't a single other creature left in the garden except Horace and the mantis. Horace half-believed that the eviction of the garden's residents was a result of the mantis' prayers.

'You are a wonderful assistant, Mantis,' said Horace to the praying mantis that evening. The mantis had grown almost as large as him, and Horace didn't notice his large eyes staring at him in a hungry sort of way. 'But why do you pray so much? I don't pray at all!' He laughed.

'Say your prayers, Horace,' whispered the mantis.

Horace stopped laughing. 'What's that you said?' The mantis had spoken for the first time.

'Say your prayers, lizard,' said the Mantis quietly. 'You're going to be my dinner.'

Horace squealed in terror and tried to escape, but the mantis caught him, fast as lightning. 'I thought you were praying all the time,' wailed Horace.

'I was preying on my victims, not praying,' smiled the mantis, as he leapt to bite the lizard.

And that was the end of the Garden Guardian.

Does the praying mantis really look like it's praying?

Yes, it does!

The praying mantis is an insect that gets its name from the long and prominent front legs that it possesses, which are bent and held together like folded hands – a gesture often used while praying. Mantises are part of a smaller group within the 'Mantids', of which there are about 1,800 species in the world.

These insects have triangular heads poised on a long 'neck', and can turn their heads 180 degrees to survey their surroundings. Their two large compound eyes have three small simple eyes between them. Though they seem like innocent, calm herbivores that stay still for long periods, they are, in fact, bloodthirsty carnivores that capture their prey using those 'praying' forelegs! These front legs have rows of spines that help to pin down the prey. Praying mantises eat moths, crickets, spiders, flies and grasshoppers, and the really large mantids can eat even frogs, lizards and small birds! The mantids use lightning-quick reflexes, which are not even visible to the naked eye, to catch their prey.

The Chinese were so impressed with the mantis that martial art forms were developed in China based on the movements and fighting strategies of the praying mantis. Praying mantis kung fu includes several styles, including Northern Praying Mantis, Southern Praying Mantis and Imperial Praying Mantis.

5

THE BLUE-EYED BOYS OF AUSTRALIA

It was September. The forests off the eastern coast of Australia were buzzing with excitement. It was that time of year again, when love was in the air for the satin bowerbirds. The yellow, green and red hues in the forest added to the charm. The male bowerbirds were busy building their 'bowers' or shady nests on the ground, because that was the only way they could impress the females. Whenever a male built a beautiful bower, with lots of added decorations, a female bird would come and inspect it, and if she liked it, she would consent to stay with him. It was a crazy competition among the male bowerbirds every year to build the best bower.

A group of such males were standing around and discussing their architectural plans. Each bird boasted about how he was going to build the best bower.

'I'm going to build my bower with some golden string that I found,' said one, puffing out his blue-black chest proudly.

'Ha! You think your bit of string will get the ladies to notice you?' said another one, turning his beak up at the first. 'My collection of smooth, shiny pebbles is going to be the centre of attraction!'

'You guys can dream all you like, but just wait and see how many are going to be impressed by the silver foil pieces that I'll use!' gloated yet another one.

'What about you, Kai?' said Cooper, one of the group, to a bird who had been silent throughout the conversation. 'What are you going to do?'

Kai was a very shy bowerbird who never spoke much. He was always sweet to everyone, often to the extent that he got teased and bullied for it. But that didn't mean he wasn't smart! He wasn't exactly as handsome as most of the males, but he was intelligent and resourceful.

However, his quiet demeanour deceived the others, and most birds mistook him as boring and unimpressive. He didn't like it; but he chose not to let others know that he was better than them in several ways.

While most birds spent their time talking and bragging, Kai worked hard and showed his prowess through his actions – he could build intricate and sturdy nests, dance better than anyone else and mimic any sound that he heard. Yet, no one, except his best friend, Cooper, recognized his talent and took him seriously.

Kai had hardly heard anything of the discussion among the male birds as he had been lost in his dreams. And now that Cooper was asking him his opinion out of the blue, Kai blushed with embarrassment.

'I, uh...do I have to say...?' he stammered, a little startled. 'I don't really have a well-formed plan...'

'Out with it, Kai,' said Cooper, grinning mischievously. 'What's up?'

'Umm...I would like to marry the princess herself,' Kai said.

The entire group, except Cooper, burst into loud peals of laughter.

'What do you think of yourself?' asked Ryan, the leader of the group. 'Here I am, the handsomest of all the males, yet I don't hope to win the princess! And what have you got to impress her?'

Kai felt hot with shame and anger. He did not show it, though. He replied in a defiant voice, 'I don't know if she will be impressed or not, but I shall marry the princess and no other!'

'We will see about that!' guffawed another, and the group started laughing again.

Cooper hurriedly dragged Kai away to another tree. 'Are you serious?' he asked.

'Of course, I am,' said Kai indignantly, 'I will not give up until I win the princess' heart!'

Cooper sighed. He didn't think it was impossible to do that – just very, very difficult. 'Understand that your goal is a tough one, Kai,' he said patiently, 'and I would not like to give you false hopes of success. But I assure you of one thing – I'm here for you, no matter what happens. I am not going to let anyone laugh at my beloved friend.' Saying this, Cooper left him to work on his bower, for the females were expected to come that way soon.

Kai set to work meticulously on his bower. He had seen the other males take dry straws alone to build their bower. But he took not only twigs and straws, but also leaves and some wire he had found near a human settlement. His bower was strong enough to withstand sun and rain.

Then he pondered over the decorations. The princess lived in comfort and had everything she could possibly want. How could he impress her then? He flew far and wide, wondering what the princess would like.

He collected some coloured glass pieces from a dump yard; broken toys lying in a park; green marbles, ribbons and coloured thermocol balls that he managed to pick up from the venue of a birthday party in the nearby town; and finally, leaves and flowers of all the colours he could find in the forest.

He decorated his home carefully. His home was nothing like that of the other bowerbirds. It was bedecked with all kinds of trimmings and looked beautiful. He eagerly stuck his head out whenever he heard a flutter of wings, hoping it was the princess.

Meanwhile, the princess had heard about Kai's open declaration of love for her, and she was quite amused. Curious to see what he had prepared, she made her way to Kai's bower. He was overjoyed. He strutted and danced, and invited the princess into his home. Cooper was watching the drama from a distance. He hoped fervently that the princess would like his friend.

Well, the princess was impressed by Kai's efforts. She slowly walked around the bower, inspecting the arrangements. She found them tasteful and ingenious, yet she wanted something unique that no other bird had. She stepped out of the bower, a little disappointed. But by now, she was moved by Kai's sincerity and wanted to give him a chance. She moved away a little farther, within hearing distance for Cooper, knowing very well that he was Kai's friend, and said, 'Oh, if only I had something blue!'

Cooper, who heard this, lost no time in flying over to Kai, who was now disappointed and glum. 'You silly bird, get something blue for your nest before someone else does!' Cooper hissed, and Kai immediately rushed off to find the right thing.

He flew all over the forest, but couldn't find a single thing that was blue, except blueberries. He winged it to the nearby town. He was thrilled by what he saw – there were little blue marbles that children played with in the streets; blue labels and papers that were strewn on the road after a recent meeting; and blue bottle caps and blue plastic rings from around the necks of water bottles. He collected all that he

could and rushed back to his bower to redecorate his home.

The princess, who had been watching from afar, now came over once again to inspect Kai's home.

Kai waited on tenterhooks.

'I think,' said the princess slowly, 'you have done very well.' Kai waited eagerly for the verdict. 'But,' she said, 'you needed a hint from me.'

Kai's heart sank again.

'However, you did everything just for me,' the princess spoke again, smiling, 'and my answer is yes.'

Kai whooped in joy and flew a loop in the air, joined by a happy Cooper, as the other bowerbirds looked on enviously, wishing they hadn't laughed at the future king of their tribe!

Do male bowerbirds really decorate their nests with blue objects?

Yes, they do!

Satin bowerbirds are medium-sized birds found along the eastern and south-eastern coast of Australia. The males have a shiny coat of bluish-black feathers, a bluish-white beak, and bright violet-blue eyes. The females are olive in colour with brown wings and tail.

These birds get their name from the 'bower' built by the male bird during the mating season to attract a female. The bower is a structure with two parallel walls and a roof, and painted with a mixture of chewed vegetable matter and the bird's saliva. The male decorates its bower with blue-coloured objects, putting up this artistic display to impress females.

If a male has managed to collect a higher number of blue objects (which are otherwise rare in the forest environment), it shows his superior skill and, therefore, he has a better chance of impressing a female. On the arrival of a female, the male bird performs an elaborate dance holding one of the blue objects in his beak. If the female is impressed, she moves into the bower to show her approval.

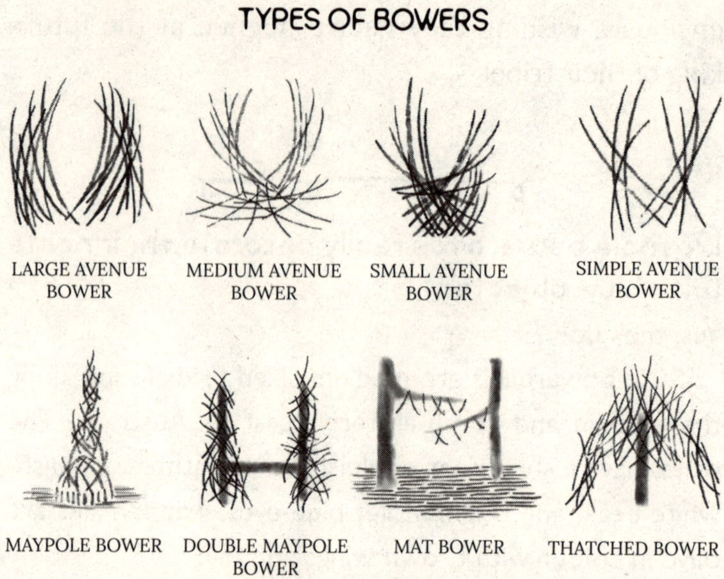

Natural-born architects, different bowerbirds construct different types of bowers

6

THE TURTLE'S QUANDARY

It was an important day in the life of Chips the turtle. Chips proudly groomed himself that morning. He had achieved his dream of becoming a postman - or rather, a post-fish - or post-turtle (since he wasn't a fish, after all) - one who delivered letters to the sea creatures. It was his first day at work.

It hadn't been easy, however; getting the postmaster — a mean whale shark — to believe that he was right for the job was a feat in itself. Though the whale shark was quite slow and had never delivered a letter in his life, he had quite a high opinion of himself. A sailfish had been the postal assistant before the turtle took up the job, and the sailfish's speed was something everyone admired. At 109 kmph, the sailfish almost flew through the water, tossing letters carelessly as he passed other fish at lightning speed. However, the sailfish had got bored of his job and left to travel the world instead. Chips, who had dreamt of nothing but this very job all his life, lost no time in applying for the vacancy.

'You're not very fast, are you?' the whale shark said at the interview, peering through his thick glasses at Chips.

'Oh, I am quite quick, sir,' said Chips eagerly. 'I can practise and become faster, if needed.'

'You don't seem very smart either,' said the whale shark, inspecting the turtle from top to bottom.

Poor Chips sat quietly, nervous and fidgeting. 'I can't imagine why the sailfish had to go off like that, putting me in trouble here,' grumbled the whale shark, taking off his glasses.

He glanced at the other candidates for the post, waiting in line for the interview. There was a seahorse, which was happily playing with a reed, a grim-looking sawfish who looked like it would slice off anyone's head, and a scowling puffer fish who had inflated itself threateningly.

'And what do I get when I advertise for the post? A list of buffoons!' muttered the whale shark to himself. Chips continued to look eagerly at the postmaster. 'Alright, look here,' said the whale shark at last, 'you don't seem bad. But I might just make up my mind not to take anyone at all.'

Chips panicked. 'Oh no, sir, don't do that! I'll do my best, I will, I will!'

Finally, the postmaster gave him the job, but on one condition. 'On the first day, you should get all the letters delivered by sunset,' said the whale shark. 'If you don't, then you're fired!'

Chips was not in the least perturbed. This was the opportunity he had been waiting for! He danced all the way home and waited eagerly to start work.

***

Finally, the day arrived, and Chips made his way to the post office. The whale shark handed Chips a bag full of letters. 'Remember what I've told you,' he warned Chips, who took off like a rocket.

He pulled out all the letters to see the names on them. He cheered up when he saw that he knew many of them. He first set off to the north and handed over a letter to the starfish. 'Congratulations!' said the starfish. But Chips didn't have the time to stop and chat. 'See you later!' he called, before landing at the next stop, the home of a clownfish. Without going too close, he tossed the letter to the clownfish as he peeped out from among the stinging sea anemones.*

The next letter was addressed to a jellyfish. Chips was a little pensive. The jellyfish always moved in swarms and he would get hurt if he tried to break into the formation! But luckily for him, the jellyfish at the outermost ring of the swarm gladly took the letter

* Want to know more about anemones? Read the first story, 'The Clownfish's Bodyguard'!

from him and passed it inside, from one jellyfish to the other, until the right one got it.

In this way, Chips delivered most of his letters. He was getting more and more confident now. He peeped into his bag. 'Just a few letters more and I'll be done!' he thought happily.

The next letter said, 'Mr Sea Cucumber, 35, Hard Rock East, Beside Coral Reef Area, Southern Ocean'. Chips frowned. What was a sea cucumber? He tried hard to remember if he had ever seen one. He decided to ask around.

'Why, it's that big, worm-like creature,' said one fish.

'Look by those rocks,' said another. 'I usually see it lazing around there.'

Chips could make out the silhouette of a dark, big worm from afar. But when he finally reached there, it was nowhere to be seen!

'Hello?' he called. How could it have disappeared so quickly? It was too big to hide anywhere and didn't seem to have swum away either. Chips hung around for a little while, puzzled. Then he picked up the next letter, hoping to find the sea cucumber later.

The next letter said, 'Leafy Sea Dragon'. Chips had never even heard of it. He asked a swordfish passing by. 'Didn't you see her on your way? She was right there near the cluster of weeds and algae!' Chips hurried to the algal patch. But all he could see were leaves!

Dejected, he looked at the next letter. It said, 'Decorator Crab'. Where was he supposed to find this one now, he wondered. At the place mentioned in the address, not a single crab was in sight – only small stones, covered in algae and anemones.

Chips had not expected this at all! He looked at the last letter in his hand: 'Mr Peacock Flounder, White Sand, Ocean Floor'. Chips went in search of White Sand. And he found only white sand there, nothing else!

***

Chips was shocked to see that it was almost evening. The sun would set soon! Upset, he just plopped himself on the white sand-covered ocean floor and cried. He was going to lose his job! He moaned and groaned, thinking how badly he wanted to keep the job.

He cried for a long time, and then slowly, started calming down. But, surprisingly, the moans and groans continued. Startled, he looked around but could see no one. It took him a while to realize that the groans were coming from beneath him!

'Get...off...me,' came a muffled voice. Chips hurriedly moved aside and was shocked to see a creature emerging from the white sand. A peacock-blue fish was now in front of him! Chips gulped a few times and asked, 'Are you the peacock flounder?'

'Yes, I am,' groaned the fish, rubbing his back. 'What's wrong with you? Why were you sitting on top of me?'

Chips was annoyed. 'I didn't even know you were there,' he said. 'And I came looking for you, but couldn't see you anywhere!'

'That's my way of hiding from both my enemies and my prey,' the fish said. 'I change my colours to match my surroundings. It's called camouflage, in case you didn't know! Why were you looking for me anyway?'

'I'm the new postal assistant,' said Chips. 'I came to give you this letter.'

The peacock flounder thanked him and was about to go back to hiding when Chips stopped him. 'Help me find the others too,' he pleaded.

The peacock flounder, being a master of disguise himself, had no problem finding all the other missing recipients. He went to one of the stones covered in sponge and seaweed and sharply rapped at it. 'Enough of the Christmas decorations. Show yourself – here's a letter for you.' To Chips's surprise, one of the stones turned out to be the decorator crab!

He next dragged out a bunch of leaves from among the algae and seaweed that Chips had seen earlier. 'Let me introduce you to the leafy sea dragon,' he said. Chips was amazed.

Finally, the flounder took Chips to the rocks. 'Come on out, cucumber,' he called. 'Chips has come to give you a letter.' Chips was startled to find something squeezing itself out of a very, very narrow crevice in the rocks, till it took on its full form of a big worm.

The sun was setting. 'And you're done!' declared the peacock flounder.

Chips thanked him and hurried back to the post office. 'I did it,' he panted.

'I suppose I can't turn you out now, can I?' said the postmaster, scowling.

And that's how Chips made his dream a reality!

Can sea creatures really disguise themselves?

Yes, they can and they do!

Sea creatures have interesting methods of hunting and defence, and 'camouflage' is one of them. Creatures like the sea cucumber have soft cylindrical bodies made of a protein called 'collagen', which they can loosen or tighten as they like, making them able to squeeze through even the narrowest of spaces! Decorator crabs use materials from their environment to cover themselves and hide from predators. The leafy sea dragon is a fish that has long, leaf-like protrusions on its body, helping it blend with the seaweeds and algae that grow in the ocean, thus escaping detection. The peacock flounder fish can change its colours to match its background pattern and colour in as little as eight seconds! It has even been found to change its colours to match the pattern of a checkerboard it was placed on! Though these are just a few creatures, there are many more in the deep sea that show such beautiful changes to survive.

7

THE TARDIGRADES SAVE THE EARTH

The sky was dark and moonless. A strange conical object, pitch black as the night, was hovering over a huge mountain somewhere in the Himalayas. The object was not immense, but about the size of a helicopter. It made no sound at all. It stood in the air silently, without support, without movement, as if waiting for something. A lone, sleepless mountain goat sensed the eerie presence in the dead of the night.

The 'thing' was in fact, a spacecraft from outer space. Humans would call it a UFO – an unidentified flying object. But of course, the goat didn't know that! It kept staring at the spaceship and bleated. 'Mehhh!'

A little while later, a bright red laser beam shone into the sky from behind the rocks on the mountain. The beam flickered for a moment and then landed on the outer body of the flying object, reflecting a dull metallic gleam.

As the mountain goat looked on in amazement, the spaceship moved in the direction of the rocks, and a small door slid open at the bottom of the metallic cone. A vertical rod emerged, descended downwards, and latched on to something. It then drew back rapidly, and the door shut. The craft started rotating. The slow spin suddenly whirred into breakneck speed, and it disappeared! The frightened goat ran away, bleating away in the soundless night.

Yet, inside the spacecraft, nothing was still or silent. There was a flurry of activity, and strange, blue-skinned creatures wearing lab coats and conical caps, were busy working in laboratories which held several strange instruments, meters and display screens. The creatures were short, had rough scaly skin, flat identical faces with three eyes bulging out, and claw-like hands and legs. One of them, who had just entered, rushed towards an inner cabin, holding something in his hand. He burst open into a room, speaking in a strange language of grunts and whistles, but this was what he said:

'Master! Master! I've got a sample,' he panted.

Another of their kind, who was sitting on a pedestal made of a shiny material, slowly looked up.

'ZK-23, what took you so long?' said the 'Master'. 'You know we don't have enough time!'

'I am sorry, Master,' mumbled ZK-23, bowing awkwardly before him.

'Time is of the essence here – if we Zoinks have to survive, we need to find another planet that we can make our home soon,' sighed the Master. 'How much fuel do we have left in our spacecraft?'

'We can travel another 50 million light years, Master,' said ZK-23.

'Well, that should last us till we find another planet, just in case Earth doesn't work out for us,' the Master said. 'But it should – I've heard that, unlike our Mother Planet that hosts only us Zoinks, Earth supports a huge variety of life forms. But still, it is dominated by the human species, which is as foolish as it is intelligent. It shouldn't be difficult for a highly advanced species like us to completely exterminate them!'

'Are we going to kill all the humans, Master? That's a huge task! The entire planet is populated with these *Homo sapiens*!'

'Not just the humans, but every form of life on Earth,' replied the Master. 'We Zoinks are used to having an entire planet to ourselves, and it will be too much to have to adjust with any other creature, however small or insignificant. Anyway, we should be thankful that there is enough nitrogen here in the earth's atmosphere for us to breathe!'

'Oh yes, Master – 78 per cent of it is nitrogen!' said ZK-23 gleefully.

'Now, hurry and analyse the sample,' ordered the Master. 'See what living forms you get, and try out those tests on them to see how they can be destroyed!' ZK-23 hurried to the laboratory.

***

The aliens in the lab worked earnestly for half an hour, while the Master waited restlessly. Finally, ZK-23 walked in, breathless as usual.

'Master, we have found a small...small...organism,' he said, nervous with excitement and apprehension. 'We want you to see it!'

'What is it?' The Master rushed into the laboratory and looked at the huge display screen, which showed what was placed under the microscope. On the screen, they could see an eight-legged, segmented organism swimming around slowly. It looked like a bear, only several times smaller.

'This is not a human!' exclaimed the Master.

'No, it is not, Master,' said ZK-23. 'But I hacked into one of the human data systems to find out its name. They call it a "tardigrade".'

'Well,' said the Master impatiently. 'What about it?'

'We don't know yet,' said ZK-23, hesitating. 'The human electronic systems are not as weak as we thought. They could detect our presence, and I was worried we would be found out. So I had to stop immediately.'

'Ah, never mind,' said the Master. 'Conduct our tests on it. Meanwhile, collect some more samples from the other points. If everything is clear, in the next 12 hours, we shall attack Earth.'

'Yes, Master,' said ZK-23. In the next five minutes, the spacecraft stopped at the Amazon rainforest, Antarctica and the Pacific Ocean, and collected samples from each place.

ZK-23 rushed back to the lab, where fellow Zoinks were waiting, all three eyes flashing with worry. They reported the results of the first test to him. He listened, nodded and handed over the fresh samples to them, ordering them to carry on with the experiments.

***

In a while, they came back to him, now looking quite troubled. After a short discussion, ZK-23 went to meet the Master.

'There is some bad news, Master,' said ZK-23. 'Those... those tardigrades that we found...in the mountain ice sample...they are also present in the other samples I took from various other places on Earth.'

'That's okay, as long as we can get rid of them – what do the test results show?' asked the Master.

'I'm sorry, Master, but the tardigrades have been able to withstand temperatures up to 150°C, and as low as -272°C,' said ZK-23.

'What? Impossible!' said the Master, shocked. 'Even we can't stand such extreme temperatures! But never mind, try ionizing radiation – now!'

A little later, ZK-23 returned. 'They are able to survive even after exposure to 5,70,000 rad units of radiation,' he said. 'X-rays, UV rays, cosmic rays... nothing seems to work!'

'Try huge amounts of pressure – extreme pressure!' shouted the Master. He was panicking now.

ZK-23 came back, shaking his head in despair. 'We put them in vacuum,' he gulped. 'And took them out – and they're still alive after that.'

Another Zoink joined the meeting. 'And a sixth of their DNA is foreign DNA,' he said, 'which means they are highly adaptable.'

'In short,' said ZK-23, 'they are impossible to kill.'

The Master looked pensive. 'But we need Earth at any cost! And we can't share our new planet with anyone!' he groaned.

'If I may suggest something, Master,' said ZK-23 timidly. 'I would say...let's leave Earth alone. I don't think we will be able to destroy all the life on this planet. We might end up bringing forth our own doom.'

'Why do you say that?' asked the Master in surprise.

'Well, Master, these organisms are so tough that none of our trials have been able to kill them. If such tiny organisms are so strong and can survive the most extreme of conditions, just imagine how much stronger the larger creatures must be? Needless to say, even the humans must be much smarter than we've heard!'

The Master thought for a while. 'You're right, ZK-23,' he said, finally. 'Let's not take a risk. There are so very few of us left anyway. Let's try to find another suitable planet soon.'

The black, conical spacecraft did not stay on the Earth a moment longer. It sped into space at the speed of light. So, quite obviously, when the mountain goat tried telling his herd the next day about the object that he had seen in the sky the previous night, they all laughed at him.

'Dreaming as usual,' sniggered one.

'He loves telling tales,' laughed another. 'But we are not going to believe them!'

The poor mountain goat didn't know how to convince his friends. The tardigrades, living in the snowy soils, smiled to themselves as they heard the commotion, but silently carried on with their lives.

Are tardigrades really so tough?

Yes, they are!

Tardigrades or water bears are one of the toughest organisms created by Nature. These water-dwellers have a barrel-shaped body and eight legs. They are around 0.1–1.5 mm in length. Though they are usually found on lichens and mosses, they are found in a variety of places including the ocean, mountain tops, rainforests and the Poles.

From battling temperature extremes, bearing pressure up to six times greater than that in the deepest ocean trenches, to surviving ionizing radiation of up to 570,000 rads and exposure to toxic chemicals, tardigrades can withstand anything! What's more, they can survive even in vacuum, in outer space – which was observed when they were launched into space on the FOTON-M3 spacecraft in 2007 by Russia! In short, they can survive conditions otherwise fatal for all other life forms.

Though these organisms need water to flourish, they can go without food or water for up to 30 years, and rehydrate themselves when conditions are favourable.

Scientists have also found that one-sixth of their DNA comes from foreign organisms – through a process called 'horizontal gene transfer', where they pick up bits and pieces of DNA from other species.

However, these creatures are not made to *live* long in extreme conditions and can only *survive* unfavourable conditions. Thus, their chances of survival decrease with increasing time of exposure to extreme conditions. Tardigrades survive by a phenomenon called 'cryptobiosis' – where they freeze or dry out completely to achieve a death-like state – where they don't move, eat or breathe – but are not actually dead. Their bodies just stop their regular functions for a time, and they can reverse their condition to normal when conditions are favourable. When they dry out, they replace almost all the water in their bodies by a sugar called 'trehalose' which protects their membranes and tissues.

The earliest known drawing (from 1773) of a tardigrade by German zoologist Johann August Ephraim Goeze, who first described what he called 'Kleiner Wasserbär' or 'little water-bears'

8

A DOSE OF YOUR OWN MEDICINE

Gloom had descended on the poison dart frogs living in the rainforests of Colombia, South America. Despite the bright colours of their skins – purple, orange, green and blue – their faces were dull and their expressions ranged from annoyed to outright angry.

An old frog sighed heavily. 'Our secret has been stolen,' he said. 'I'm sure there must be a traitor in our midst who gave it away!' His piercing eyes stared suspiciously at all the frogs assembled there.

'Those foul birds are getting all the credit now!' complained another frog. 'Oh...how I hate them!'

The cause of their distress was that a scientist had discovered that birds called the hooded pitohui, found in New Guinea off the coast of Australia, had poison similar to that of the poison dart frogs, in their bodies, skin and feathers. That made them one of the very few poisonous bird species in the world.

The frogs had earlier enjoyed the unique status of being the only creatures producing 'batrachotoxin', a poison that was several times stronger than many toxins in the world, and helped them kill any predator that tried to harm them.

I wonder how they could get our secret, though, thought a tiny young frog, who was sitting on a leaf a little higher than the rest of the gathering. 'They stay so far…9,500 miles away!' he said aloud. 'On a different continent too! Maybe they're innocent after all.'

A huge croak of protest rose up in the air. Some of the larger frogs charged at him, while some of the females screamed in horror.

'How dare you support those birds!' the old frog said menacingly. 'Are *you* the traitor?'

'No, no, of course not,' squeaked the poor little frog, whose neck was now held in an iron grip by a large blue-black frog.

'Just a baby, and blabbering away as if he knows everything!' snapped the old frog. 'And if you want to know how they might have spied on us, let me remind you: they are birds, and they can fly!'

The large frog released his grip on the tiny frog, who rubbed his neck in relief. He decided it was better to keep his mouth shut.

'Can't you see your elders sitting down here?' shouted the old frog. 'Who said you could sit on a higher branch when your seniors are holding a meeting here? You better come down, this instant!'.

The tiny frog meekly came down and made himself as inconspicuous as possible, which was quite difficult, since every frog was now looking at him disapprovingly.

'I propose we file a lawsuit against them,' said a frog with huge, bulging eyes. 'Our poison, our venom, belongs to us. We were the first to be known as the ones using this bat...bat...batra...'

'Batrachotoxin!' piped up the tiny frog, quite forgetting his earlier disgrace. All the frogs frowned at him, and he whispered, 'Uh, sorry.'

The bulgy-eyed frog continued, 'Yes, yes, the batrachotoxin... We should be the only ones with the right to use it! We should be the sole owners of our toxin! We can't let these flying upstarts, these hooded whatchamacallits, to produce the same toxin as us and get away with it!'

The old frog nodded gravely. Shouts of agreement greeted the bulgy-eyed frog who dashed off a legal notice to the hooded pitohuis, and other letters of complaint to several scientists around the world. 'That's going to put them in their place, alright!' he said, rubbing his webbed forelimbs in glee.

***

The hooded pitohuis were quite surprised when they received a legal notice accusing them of having stolen the frogs' secret formula for making poison. They hadn't even been aware that the poison dart frogs of South America produced the same kind of poisonous compound! All they knew was that they had been blessed with an ability to ward off their bigger predators like the hawk, who would otherwise have never thought twice before gobbling them up!

'We never asked anyone to give us any publicity,' grumbled the chief of the hooded pitohui birds. 'Now just look at all the trouble we are having!'

'I say, let's send them a notice back saying it's the scientists who said it, not we,' said another pitohui bird.

'Or, better still, let's all fly there and eat up those teeny-tiny frogs!' said another pitohui.

'And then be accused of terminating a species?' asked their leader. 'As it is, I don't think it's very nice to be called the only poisonous bird in the world. It feels like a bad tag.'

'Alright then, let's wait for the scientists to clear our name,' said another bird. 'We did nothing, to begin with.' And that settled the matter for the pitohuis.

The frogs, however, were quite restless. When would the birds respond? What would they say? What were the scientists doing? But to their great relief, a few months later, the scientists came up with another discovery: the poison was not produced by

the hooded pitohui birds after all! It was produced by the Choresine beetles, which the hooded pitohuis ate, and the toxins then piled up in the birds' skin and feathers.

The frogs went crazy with joy. 'Aha! Now they can't claim to be the "bird" producers of our deadly poison!'

The hooded pitohuis were more than relieved. Their chief sent a message to the leader of the Choresine beetles, asking if she would like to publish any claim regarding their toxin. The leader of the beetles said they couldn't be bothered with such things, as they had more important things to do, like saving themselves from being eaten by the pitohui birds.

But the bulgy-eyed frog wasn't satisfied. He now wanted to file a lawsuit against the Choresine beetles for producing the toxin.

'Forget it,' said the old frog. 'How will we find all the poisonous insects in the world and file lawsuits against them?'

'I don't know how, but I will do it. It is our right, our sole right...' And the bulgy-eyed frog started off another speech that held the rest of the frogs spellbound. Just then, the tiny frog came in, interrupting him, 'Look at this! It's a letter addressed to us frogs!'

That was a surprise! Who could have written them a letter now? 'Must be a letter of congratulations, no doubt,' said the bulgy-eyed frog smugly.

'This is what it says,' said the tiny frog, reading it out aloud:

Poison dart frogs,

Stop claiming that batrachotoxin is produced by you. You may be unaware that, similar to the pitohui birds, you get your toxin from us insects whom you eat every day. If you're not careful, we will file a lawsuit against you.

– The beetles of the Amazon rainforest

Do poisonous birds really exist?

Yes, they do!

The hooded pitohui (*Pitohui dichrous*) birds of New Guinea are one of the few known poisonous birds in the world. However, they were the first poisonous birds to be identified and documented. With beautiful orange and black plumage, these attractive songbirds are not as cute as they look! Their feathers and skin contain batrachotoxin – a deadly poison that affects the nervous system upon contact.

The bright colours on their body also act as a warning signal to their enemies, a phenomenon called 'aposematism' [say *ap-uh-sey-muh-tism*]. However, the birds themselves do not produce the toxin – they obtain it from the Choresine beetles, which they eat, and are immune to the poison themselves. This is a form a chemical defence that birds have evolved to escape their predators. Two other birds – belonging to the genus *Ifrita* and *Colluricincla* – also contain the same poison in their bodies.

The poison dart frogs (belonging to the genus *Phyllobates*) of Colombia, South America, also obtain the deadly batrachotoxin the same way, by eating beetles and other insects that produce the venom. Poison dart frogs bred in a lab on a normal diet are found to be harmless, with no traces of the toxin in their bodies, thus showing that the source of the poison is external.

9

SNOW WHITE AND THE SEVEN CODS

Once upon a time, around 25 million years ago, lived a codfish in the waters of the Pacific Ocean. This little codfish was quite different from the others of her kind – she was born a washed-out white, without scales, and white as snow in some parts and almost transparent in others, which made the other little codfish avoid her.

It was quite evident that she did not have the same red blood running through her veins as the other fish in her group, who all had solid flesh and scales in colours of grey, green and brown. So this particular codfish – let's call her Snow White – had to fend for herself. It was a big struggle for her, especially as she was not only pale in colour, but weak as well. She found it difficult to breathe in enough oxygen, and the warm water currents they lived in made it worse for her. It took her an enormous amount of willpower and strength to just survive.

Snow White was a good-natured fish who was polite, kind and cheerful, but no one was prepared to see her good qualities. All they saw was that she was strange, different, and struggling with some unknown malady. The snails withdrew into their shells when they saw her coming, and the octopus rolled up his eight arms as if he was scared of touching her by mistake. Some of the other fish stared at her as she passed by.

The other codfish, of course, gave her the silent treatment, swimming away swiftly the moment they saw her approaching. Though there was nothing wrong with her, the other fish didn't want to risk being seen with her, lest they too be avoided by the rest of the group!

Her troubles increased when she was spotted in an area just before a fishing trawler came by, trapping several fish of their group. This happened multiple times in different places in the ocean, purely by chance – but she was then branded as unlucky by not just the codfish, but all the sea creatures in the vicinity! They started making snarky comments and criticizing Snow White whenever she was within earshot, hoping they could make her leave their part of the ocean of her own accord.

Snow White silently put up with all the harsh treatment from the others. She knew there was no point arguing with those who had already made up their mind about her. She put on a brave face and hoped there would be a day when her 'unlucky' appearance would become lucky for her.

***

Then, one day, things started going terribly wrong for all the creatures of the ocean. It started getting colder and colder with each passing day. Many of the smaller fish died, and the other fish had a hard time coping up with the cold. There were, of course, a few who seemed more comfortable with the chill in the waters, but most of them were unhappy with the dropping temperatures. The sea creatures discussed what the cause could be for such a misfortune.

'This sort of thing has never happened before,' said a young codfish, with a superior air of one who had lived through the entire history of the earth and oceans.

'Don't talk about things you don't know, sonny,' said a crab. 'It has happened before, but many, many years ago...long before you were born.'

'Well, why did it happen then?' demanded a starfish. 'There must be a reason!'

'It must have been the presence of another fish like Snow White,' said a malicious codfish. 'That must have turned the tide towards ill fortune!'

'She is the harbinger of calamity', said another codfish. 'Remember the times the fishing trawler appeared when she was nearby?'

The fish started whispering among themselves. Now everybody found this the most acceptable explanation, one that they were comfortable with. They hated to think that anyone else, other than Snow White, could be responsible for the disaster.

'Snow White must be brought before the Seven Cod Council!' cried a codfish.

This council was a group of seven codfish who judged wrongdoers. These fish belonged to the oldest clan of codfish in the region, revered for having the best features passed down to them by their ancestors. They were very powerful, sometimes ruthless, and no fish dared to even cross their path.

'Yes, she must be punished for bringing bad luck to our ocean!' said another fish.

Very soon, all the fish started demanding the Seven Cod Council to hold court.

Snow White was unaware of all that was happening. So when a swordfish came to tell her that she was being summoned by the Seven Cod Council, she was both surprised and afraid. 'Why am I being called?' she cried. 'What have I done?'

The swordfish refused to answer. He felt he had already invited enough bad luck by talking once to her. Dreading what was going to come, Snow White followed him to the reef clearing where the seven codfish of the council were sitting on high mounds on the ocean bed, with a central clearing in the middle.

Snow White waited silently there, with the seven cods glaring down at her.

'We have found that you are responsible for the changing temperature of the ocean,' said the oldest of the seven, his gaze steady on her. 'And we believe you need to be punished for bringing such rotten luck upon us.'

'If any sea creature has any objection, I ask him or her to voice it now!' thundered the second codfish of the council. Not a single creature moved. The hydra opened her mouth to say something, then thought better of it and shut it again.

'No one seems to have any objection, Snow White,' said the third codfish softly. 'In that case, we shall pronounce your sentence.'

Snow White trembled and wondered what was coming. 'You are banished to the ice-cold Southern Ocean,' came the booming voice of the second codfish again. 'You should not be seen here ever again!'

No fish could survive in the freezing waters of the Southern Ocean.

But no sooner did the codfish pass the sentence than the audience rose to corner Snow White. 'Go now!' they cried. 'Go away!'

Snow White had no option but to flee. She swam faster and faster, crying all the way. She hardly knew where she was going. She swam on and the waters started getting terribly cold, colder than she'd ever known them to be. But strangely, she did not feel uncomfortable, and could breathe freely through her soft gills and ultra-thin skin. In fact, she felt better than she had ever felt all her life! With a shock, she realized it was her body without the red blood that seemed to be helping her survive the harsh, freezing cold.

Then she spotted several other fish, swimming away in the cold waters. To her surprise and joy, she realised that many of them looked like her! With a cry of joy, she joined them – they came to be known as the icefish, for their ability to survive in the icy cold waters of the Antarctic.

Snow White survived that Ice Age, as the cold that had come creeping on them had not been brought on by her, but by the earth itself, in one of its many glacial cycles.

As for the other fish in the warm waters, who had banished Snow White, they froze away along with the earth, and the few that survived had to move away elsewhere, trying to adjust to the new climatic conditions. Snow White had survived, just because she was...different.

How do icefish in oceans near the Poles survive?

Antarctic icefish are starkly different from most vertebrates, and most fish too, in the fact that they do not have haemoglobin – the red colouring pigment in our red blood cells, which carries oxygen taken in through the lungs to the different cells and organs in the body. Antarctic icefish are the only vertebrates that lack both red blood cells and haemoglobin.

In fact, the loss of haemoglobin in these fish occurred by accident at the genetic level, forcing the icefish to alter their body to survive, as their colourless blood can transport only 10 per cent of the oxygen compared to other fish. Though the onset of the Ice Age occurred later, it eventually turned out advantageous for them as they adapted themselves to the changing environment. Their thin blood helped them survive in the cold currents around Antarctica, as thinner blood can circulate more easily, an advantage in harsh conditions.

Yet, how could they prevent their blood from freezing, when the Arctic waters themselves drop below -2°C? (The water doesn't freeze at 0°C as salts dissolved in the ocean lower its freezing point.) The answer is anti-freeze glycoproteins (a combination of carbohydrate and protein) in the blood, which bind to the tiny water crystals that start forming in the blood when the temperature drops below freezing point. By binding to these crystals, the anti-freeze proteins (AFPs) prevent the ice from building up, saving the fish from getting frozen.

The AFPs were first discovered in the icefish in the 1960s by American biologist Arthur DeVries. Later in the 1980s, it was found that several fungi, bacteria and plants also contain anti-freeze glycoproteins that help them survive extreme cold.

10

BATTLING BERIBERI WITH ANOTHER B

Dr Kanehiro stood on the deck, looking at the raging waves of the North Pacific Ocean. It looked like he had failed.

'Doctor, Doctor,' a voice called. One of the ship's crew came running to him. 'Another soldier has taken ill,' he informed. 'Please have a look at him, Doctor.'

Kanehiro sighed. It was of no use. How could he treat the patients without knowing what was causing their disease? He had looked at all their blood samples and had examined them in detail, but in vain. The cause of the disease still eluded him. 'I shall come in a while,' he told the man, and headed for the captain's cabin. He had to tell the captain that he had given up. It would be better if they brought in someone else in his place.

The captain was, however, in no mood to listen to Kanehiro's tale of woe. 'Ah, come in, Doctor,' he said jovially, a drink in his hand. 'I believe you've not met my good friends, the merchants who trade in stones and spices and travel to mysterious lands,' he said, waving his hand at the gathering of well-dressed gentlemen, who were enjoying the captain's hospitality.

'Captain, I came to say that—'

'Is it about that fellow mumbling beriberi? Is he dead? Don't bother, that fellow was never very good anyway. We just got a fancy name for that disease of theirs, though!' he chuckled, while his friends laughed. 'I just hope we don't catch it.'

'But, Captain—'

'Oh, we can discuss everything after lunch – the steward just informed me that we have a feast waiting for us,' the captain cut Kanehiro short and took him along with the others. Kanehiro had no option but to follow.

At the table, a spread awaited them. Meat, fruits, vegetable stew, fried fish, and of course, white rice were laid out in a delicious array. Kanehiro could hardly eat, while the captain and his friends ate with gusto. Kanehiro quickly finished his lunch, mumbled an apology for leaving the table early and walked out. He went down to the kitchen of the deckhands and the soldiers, his guilt weighing him down. If the captain wouldn't listen, he at least had to inform the poor soldiers whose mates were suffering and dying.

When he reached their dining area, he was greeted by sounds of welcome. The crew were overwhelmed by his visit to their humble dining cabin. 'Hey, get a plate of good food for the doctor,' called one. 'Not just rice, you fool, look for something else—'

'Dr Kanehiro, you are our saviour here on board this cursed ship,' said another of the crew, while a seaman poured him a drink.

Kanehiro looked curiously at what they were all eating. Every plate had a mound of cooked white rice, but nothing else. He took a few of the grains in his hands. 'Isn't this polished white rice?' Kanehiro asked the steward.

'Yes, sir, it is,' the man informed.

'Don't you get anything else to eat?' asked Kanehiro.

'Sir, this is the only thing that we get free aboard the ship,' he replied. 'We poor soldiers can't afford to pay for the fruits or the meat.'

As Kanehiro made his way back to his own cabin, he was lost in thought. Why were only the poor soldiers afflicted, and not the captain or the rich merchants? It must be the food! Maybe the nutrition wasn't enough. Maybe...

The captain was surprised when Kanehiro knocked at his door that afternoon. 'I have a solution,' he said firmly.

***

Meanwhile, in Java (now in Indonesia), it was quite the other way around. The settlers from Holland, who were a part of the Dutch East India Company were a privileged lot but were suffering from beriberi.

Surprisingly, the poor people of the land hardly had anything to eat, but were safe from the disease.

And that was where a messenger came in search of Dr Christiaan Eijkman, a doctor at a hospital. One of the assistants there led him outside instead of taking him to the doctor's cabin.

'Hey, where are you taking me?' he asked. 'I want to see the doctor, not the caretaker!'

Dr Eijkman was carefully feeding the chickens in the hen coop, when the assistant arrived with the messenger. 'Here, eat this...' he was saying, as he threw some brown rice on the floor. The chickens rushed over to peck at the grains, flapping their wings. Then he went to the next hen coop and threw some white

rice on the ground. The chickens didn't move. Some looked lethargic and some looked like they were about to collapse. A few moved forward slowly and started pecking at the rice.

'Are you sure that's the doctor?' asked the messenger dubiously. 'What's he doing with the chickens? Shouldn't he be inside looking after the patients?'

The assistant shrugged. 'Lost his marbles, I suppose,' he said. 'As crazy as the patients with beriberi in there.'

The doctor looked up and saw the messenger. 'Ah, you must be carrying the message from the medical panel,' he said, and eagerly reached out for the letter in the man's hand. He tore it open and read it, and cursed under his breath.

'Why can't he see it?' He stomped his foot on the ground angrily and hopped around in fury. He suddenly caught hold of the startled messenger's arm and dragged him to the hen coop.

'Look here – what do you see?' he asked in a threatening voice.

'Uh...chickens?' said the bewildered messenger, unsure where this was going.

'They're the chickens I am experimenting on,' Dr Eijkman said proudly. 'Do you see those healthy chickens there? I have been feeding them brown rice. And you see those sick ones? They have been eating white rice. Now do you see the difference? It's in the rice! Rather, in the brown husk of the rice! And that's what we've been missing! Why can't the director understand? We should be eating the brown rice! And the disease can be wiped out. There's no infection, no bacteria responsible for this!'

He tore the letter to shreds and stamped on them. The messenger hurried away. 'That doctor's stark raving mad,' he whispered to the assistant whom he met on the way out.

It wasn't long before Eijkman was packed off back home. 'How dare he suggest that we eat brown rice, the rice of the poor natives!' fumed the director of the medical panel.

But the director had to eat his words – and perhaps brown rice too! – when Dr Eijkman received nothing less than the Nobel Prize for his discovery of Vitamin B1, which is also called 'thiamine' – that is present in the brown husk of rice!

What is beriberi?

Beriberi is a disease caused by thiamine (vitamin B1) deficiency. It affects a variety of organs and systems of the body, including the nervous system, digestive system, heart and muscles. If untreated, it can be fatal. The name 'beriberi' comes from the Sinhalese language, for 'I cannot' – it signifies the weakness and helplessness of the afflicted patients.

Thiamine (or thiamin) is one of the B vitamins – a group of chemically distinct, water-soluble vitamins that also includes riboflavin, niacin, pantothenic acid, pyridoxine, biotin, folic acid and others. Thiamine is essential in small amounts for human health as it plays a role in extracting energy from glucose, proteins and fats. It does this by participating in a process called the 'Krebs Cycle' in cells. Also, it is needed for normal growth and development, and proper functioning of the organs.

Thiamine, being water-soluble, easily dissolves in water, and is excreted through urine. Only a very small amount of it is stored in the liver, and no longer than 18 days. It is therefore necessary to replenish our reserves of thiamine through our diet. Among good sources of thiamine are various vegetables, including legumes and green peas, as well as liver, nuts and yeast. The aleurone layer (an outer layer) of unpolished rice is a rich source.

Thiamine was first discovered in 1910 in Japan, as a result of research into how rice bran cured patients of beriberi. Until that time, it was a mystery why beriberi was affecting so many people of all ages in Asia, and only in the early 1900s was it understood that rice bran contained something to prevent it. In many Asian countries, there was a reliance on white (polished) rice as a staple food, with the removal of the bran, which contains most of the thiamine.

Dr Takaki Kanehiro was a Japanese naval medical officer, whose research showed that beriberi was caused by nutritional deficiency and helped to eradicate the disease in the Japanese Navy in the 1880s. Nearly 30 years later, Dutch physician Dr Christiaan Eijkman pointed to 'thiamine' as the missing vitamin/ nutrient. He received the Nobel Prize for Medicine in 1929, along with Sir Frederick Hopkins, for their contributions towards the discovery of vitamins.

Dr Takaki Kanehiro

Dr Christiaan Eijkman

11

A GUEST AT THE ANT NEST

It was another busy day at the Ant Nest. Ants were busy scurrying around, carrying food to and fro, taking care of their eggs and babies, and running several other errands. The commander-in-chief of the Ant Home was Major Ancy, who stood at the entrance, supervising the goings-on. He shouted instructions from time to time.

'Hey, you – yes, you – have you cleaned the south part of the nest? Well, you better, or I'll have you kicked out in a minute! Mark, buck up – you need to take care of the eggs – And you, Nelly – have you milked the aphids yet? No? What are you waiting for? Take your troop and milk them now! Our aphid farms are the most important! No neglecting them!'

The ants who had received the instructions hurried off, and only Nelly hung back.

Major Ancy frowned. 'Why are you wasting your time here? Get going!'

'Umm... I was just wondering... Do I really need to do this job? Can't I be in some other department? Cleaning, taking care of our ant eggs...anything is fine. I don't like milking the aphids or taking care of our aphid farms.'

Major Ancy gave a sarcastic smile. 'You don't like milking aphids, eh? How about stopping your supply of honeydew then? You definitely don't seem to have a problem when it comes to gobbling up food!'

Major Ancy and the others were not just any ants – they were Japanese carpenter ants who kept farms, quite like humans. Except these were farms of plant lice called aphids, which sucked out the sap of plants. The ants brought the aphid eggs home and nursed the young aphid babies when the eggs hatched. Later, when the aphids grew up and started feeding on plant sap, the ants 'milked' them for honeydew – by stroking them with their feelers. The honeydew was then collected and eaten by the ants. It was just like people milking cows.

Nelly was quite alarmed when he heard the major's threat. He didn't want to stop eating honeydew. He sped away without a word. Major Ancy snorted. Lazy ants!

Major Ancy stood around that morning, supervising the aphid eggs being brought in. Nelly scowled behind Major Ancy's back. He hardly noticed which eggs he was bringing in. He muttered grumpily under his breath about having to suffer in the aphid-care department.

***

A few days later, Nelly came running to Major Ancy again, half excited and half scared. Some other ants followed him, frightened and nervous. 'Major, Major,' Nelly said, panting, 'there's a strange creature that has hatched out of one of the eggs. I don't think it's an aphid!'

This was an emergency! Major Ancy rushed over. There lay a small worm – a caterpillar – lying quite still.

'Aaaaaaaahhhh! It's come to kill us!' cried a hysterical ant, running around in frantic circles. 'Run, everyone, it's a monster!'

'Quiet!' shouted Major Ancy. 'Let me see.'

Major Ancy went a little closer to the caterpillar. It was hardly moving. Would it eat them up? I'll never let that happen, thought Major Ancy firmly. They would all circle it and bite it to death!

He went a little closer. 'Careful, Major, careful,' whispered Nelly apprehensively.

The caterpillar suddenly turned over.

'Back, Major!' cried the horrified ants.

Major Ancy stayed as still as stone, waiting for the caterpillar's next move. But nothing happened. Major Ancy dared to move forward a little more. Then he sniffed the air. How surprising! A familiar smell seemed to be coming from the caterpillar. The creature smelt just like one of them! He went even closer. He didn't feel threatened anymore. Instead, he felt something like parental affection towards the caterpillar! He couldn't figure out why; the smell seemed to have hypnotized him. He beckoned the other ants to come closer. As they came nearer, they too felt the same hypnotizing smell.

'Hey! He's one of us!' cried Nelly.

'Yes, he's just like one of our babies!' said another.

'Let's feed him!' cried another.

Major Ancy stood by smiling like an indulgent father while the other ants fed the caterpillar. 'Take good care of him!' he barked at the other ants, who seemed happy enough to feed him.

It wasn't long before Nelly called out to the others. 'Hey, look – he's giving us honeydew!' he cried out gleefully.

Major Ancy seemed gratified. 'Well, he's one of us now...' he said. 'He's useful, so keep him well cared for.'

The other ants had a fine time competing with each other to feed their special guest who looked different but had become one of them. They liked the honeydew they got from him too. Nelly seemed to have developed an interest in his duties, probably from the novelty of the situation.

This went on for some time, till one day the caterpillar ate a few aphids from their aphid farm. The report came to Major Ancy.

'Is he still giving honeydew?' said Ancy.

'Yes, he is', said Nelly.

'Keep him,' said Major Ancy, though he was not always so tolerant. 'Shouldn't be a problem if he eats a few aphids.'

The caterpillar was moving around now, eating up the aphids as and when he could, and growing large. He was quite silent, though, and his unique smell that matched the ants' kept him safe.

***

Then, one day, at the entrance of the ant nest, he started spinning his cocoon. Before the ants could figure out what had happened, the caterpillar was safely enclosed in the cocoon.

Nelly was depressed. 'I can't feed him now,' he said morosely to anyone who would listen.

Major Ancy wasn't very bothered. 'Oh, he'll come out soon,' he said.

A few days later, the cocoon started to crack. 'My baby's coming out again!' sang Nelly, sailing around the nest in joy. 'Now I can feed him again!'

But the creature that came out was no more a caterpillar. It was a fully grown beautiful butterfly! Nelly was quite astonished, but quickly recovered. 'He's become even more gorgeous!' he raved.

Major Ancy wasn't that happy. He went closer. The butterfly no longer smelled like one of the ants! 'No! This one is a traitor!' he cried out. 'He has used us!'

All the ants rushed forward. The butterfly was preparing to fly away.

'He's getting away!' shrieked Major Ancy. 'Stop him!'

But it was too late. The ants bit at the butterfly's wings but could hardly get at him, and he seemed immune to their bites. He went away flying into the air, his pretty wings fluttering.

The entire ant nest was in shock for a few days.

'Never trust a stranger again', said Major Ancy darkly.

Many months passed. Then one day, Nelly and a few ants came carrying another caterpillar to the Ant Home. 'Major Ancy! Look what we found!' he said, grinning foolishly.

Major Ancy sniffed at the motionless caterpillar. 'He's one of us', he smiled, his face taking on an indulgent look. 'Take him in.'

What kind of butterflies are these, that fool ants to survive?

Niphanda fusca is a parasitic butterfly that belongs to the larger family of butterflies called Lycedidae, all of which depend on ants to complete their life cycle. This particular butterfly steals its nutrition from the Japanese carpenter ants (*Camponotus japonicas*), which rear aphids to collect honeydew for their own nutrition.

The female butterfly lays an egg on a plant where the ants live. Usually ants prey on caterpillars, but this caterpillar releases certain chemicals called 'pheromones', which are similar to the ant's own secretions, thus fooling them to believe that it is one of them. The ants carry the caterpillar back to their nest, where they feed it, and it gives them honeydew in return to ensure its own safety and survival.

Once the caterpillar reaches the pupal stage, it spins its cocoon at the entrance of the ant nest. A fully grown butterfly then hatches from the cocoon, at which point the ants attack it. But the butterfly's wings are woolly and do not get affected by the ant bites, and so it flies away safely.

12

ELEPHANTINE PROBLEMS

The animals of the Malaysian rainforest were in deep thought. The elder ones were frowning and the younger ones looked bewildered. Everyone was talking in low voices.

'We have to do something about these mosquitoes,' sighed the white-handed gibbon, who was otherwise quite cheery and playful.

'Our young ones can't sleep, and some of them are falling sick from the mosquito bites,' said the mouse deer.

They had all gathered to discuss their problems and look for a solution. Their usual meeting place, the lake, was now the haunt of the mosquitoes.

'The mosquito population has increased tremendously,' said the elephant.

'Even humans are not spared,' said the spot-necked bulbul. 'They are devastated by a disease called dengue, which is spread by these Aedes mosquitoes. I heard the humans say that they are going to raze the forest and spray poison on the lake to get rid of the mosquitoes!'

This bit of news from the bulbul gave everyone a shock. The younger ones started crying while the bigger animals started to panic and complain. If the forest was lost and the lake got contaminated, they would all die.

Just then, the sun bear joined them and silenced the gathering. 'QUIET!' he roared. 'What's all this about?'

An uneasy hush ruled till the red squirrel spoke up. 'We have to get rid of the mosquitoes, sun bear!' she said.

'You know the jungle laws, squirrel,' said the sun bear. 'Survival of the fittest is the rule. These mosquitoes are bothersome, but they claim that they do not kill anyone intentionally. They say they are not responsible for the diseases they spread.'

He turned to the giant stick insect, 'They are insects like you – your relatives. Can't you ask them to leave the forest?'

'Why would they listen to me?' replied the giant stick insect.

'If the mosquitoes don't stop their mischief, the humans will destroy our home!' cried the leopard. 'We will all die!'

'I have a suggestion,' said the elephant, 'I know some relatives of the mosquitoes, called the elephant mosquitoes. They can kill the Aedes mosquitoes that are bothering us.'

'What if they joined their cousins here and started biting us?' the gibbon wanted to know.

'They won't – they feed only on plant nectar,' said the elephant.

'Both the males *and* females?' asked the squirrel incredulously. In almost every other mosquito species, the females fed on mammalian blood, while the males fed on plant sap.

'Yes, both,' replied the elephant.

The other animals had never heard of the elephant mosquito, but decided to go along with the elephant, as they had no other option anyway.

The elephant and the leopard set out to the Eastern United States to meet the king of the elephant mosquitoes. They boarded a ship with the help of the monkeys, pretending in front of the humans that they were being sent to a zoo there.

Once they reached the US, they gave them the slip! They immediately went in search of the elephant mosquito king, and found him resting on a buttercup, lazily drinking from its nectar compartments from time to time. He looked quite elegant and nothing like the black or striped mosquitoes back home. His coat was a metallic colour, giving him the look of a warrior in armour. He patiently heard out the elephant.

'What's in it for me?' he asked finally.

'Free food, of course, and free shelter as well,' said the elephant.

'I get that here anyway', said the mosquito, with a bored expression.

'And you get Malaysian exotic flora to feed on,' said the elephant hastily. 'You won't get such delicious nectar elsewhere!'

'What's the guarantee that *you'll* help us?' asked the leopard, who was quite annoyed with the mosquito's insolence.

The mosquito grinned lazily. 'There's no other way we'd survive, you know,' he explained. 'Our young ones – our larvae – need protein. They get it only when they feed on other mosquito larvae. And once we are adults, well, we survive on a carb diet. Just juices and workouts – the secret to our perfect bodies.' He drew himself up to display his 'fabulous' figure.

'All right then, it's a deal,' said the elephant who couldn't stand the cool weather any longer. 'Send along your swarms with us.'

And, soon, the elephant mosquito swarms invaded the forests of Malaysia. They laid eggs in the lake, and their larvae ate up the larvae of the Aedes mosquitoes. The Aedes mosquito population dwindled, and the humans no longer wanted to destroy the forest.

The Malaysian rainforest was saved.

Does the elephant mosquito really exist?

Yes, it does!

Elephant mosquitoes belong to the genus *Toxorhynchites*. Though they are native to Eastern United States, they have been used successfully in Japan, South East Asia, the Caribbean and the rest of the US as a biological agent to control populations of *Aedes egyptii* mosquitoes, which spread the dreaded dengue fever among humans.

The elephant mosquitoes do not suck blood and instead survive on plant nectar. Their larvae feed on the larvae of other mosquito species, such as the *Aedes*.

13

MONSTER VERSUS MONSTER

Kyros sat looking out of the window at his home in Crete, his gaze fixed on the blue-green ocean waves that tumbled towards the shore. His mind was wandering elsewhere, though.

'Why doesn't anyone want any publicity here?' he muttered softly to himself. 'Everyone seems happy with a mediocre life!'

Kyros had just returned from the United States after a ten-year-long career as a public relations specialist at some of the top companies there. Public relations was all about building a good image for clients and ensuring them good publicity. He liked his job, because he could do what he did best: talk. He had the gift of the gab, and coupling it with his charm, he could convince anyone about anything. Finally, he decided to set up his own public relations company back home in Greece.

Unfortunately for him, Crete was a much quieter place. Though he advertised his services, he didn't get a single client.

His sister, Lana, who was a marine biologist, also ran a small restaurant for tourists from their home. 'This pays better,' she said. 'And, besides, who would have taken care of Grandpa? You just left everything to me and had a wonderful time in the US.' That was something she often grumbled about.

'Well, you went to Australia too, to do your research on the eerie-cutting...whatsoever that was,' he pointed out.

'Irukandji,' Lana corrected him angrily. 'Maybe, but I came back when Grandpa fell ill. You didn't!'

Kyros was still pondering over this when Lana thrust an envelope under his nose.

'It's for you,' she said, smiling. 'Looks like you're going to get some work!'

Kyros took out the letter and started to read. 'It's an offer for me all right, but look at the sum they're offering.' he said. 'Phewwwwwwwww!' he whistled, his face turning red.

'How much is it?' asked Lana. 'If it's too little, don't go.'

'No, Lana, to the contrary,' Kyros said. 'In fact, it's enough to let me spend my life in luxury.'

'Whom is it from?' asked Lana.

'Hmm...it says Medusa Gorgon,' said Kyros. 'I'm supposed to go meet her.'

'What kind of a name is that?' said Lana. 'I think it's a hoax.' But Kyros set out immediately.

***

Kyros couldn't help wondering about the sudden windfall. Could it be a fraud, like Lana had said? Nevertheless, he found the house and rang the doorbell. A voice thundered in reply, 'Who's there?'

'This is Kyros here,' he answered, 'Your brand-new publicity agent...'

The door swung open, and standing before him was a woman in old Greek robes, wearing on her head a strange paper bag that covered her face. A curious hissing noise could be heard from the bag.

'Come in,' she said. A claw-like hand emerged and caught his wrist with surprising strength. He found himself being dragged inside and shoved onto a sofa that was as hard as stone.

Kyros was startled but gathered his wits soon. He put on his most charming smile and started talking in the smooth tone that he used to floor both his friends and opponents. 'So charmed to meet you, Miss Gorgon. Let me introduce myself. You must be...'

'Enough of the chatter,' the booming voice cut him off. 'I know all about you. All I want to know is whether you can work for me. Do you know who I am?'

Kyros racked his brains. Was there a famous politician or business tycoon called Medusa Gorgon?

The woman, meanwhile, handed him a mirror and stood behind him.

'A mirror?' thought Kyros. 'She must be a movie star!'

He cleared his throat and began his smooth talk again. 'Why of course, I shall work for you, and yes, I know that you are Miss Medusa Gorgon, the famous mov...AAAAAAAHHHHH!'

Kyros screamed as he raised the mirror, for now he could see the woman in it! She had a terrible face, with greenish skin, fearsome red orbs for her eyes and, most frightening of all, instead of hair, she had numerous tiny snakes hissing and coiling around each other on her head. She was Medusa, the famous monster from Greek mythology! Kyros remained transfixed at the image, while his client coolly sat down.

'Miss Medusa Gorgon, the famous monster,' she said calmly, completing his sentence for him.

'But...but...you don't really exist!' said Kyros, not daring to take his eyes off the mirror image. 'Your place is in Greek myths and legends...'

'Ha! That's what everyone thinks!' mocked the monster. 'Medusa is just a silly story to frighten kids nowadays. But no! I do exist, and I'm here to prove it!'

Kyros trembled in fear, while Medusa wore her paper bag again. 'Now, you're going to be my publicity agent,' she drawled. 'You're going to make sure that the world knows of my existence. I want to get back my fame as the most fearsome monster in the world!'

'I…I'll try…but you know…people might not believe me,' stammered Kyros.

'I suppose you know you'll turn to stone if you look into my eyes directly?' she asked threateningly. 'Well, that's what will happen if you fail. If you succeed, well, you get your reward.'

A very shaken Kyros made his way back home.

***

'Well, how did it go?' asked Lana.

Kyros told her the entire story.

Lana laughed at him. 'Someone's made a real fool of you!'

But days passed, and Kyros wouldn't come out of the shock. Mysterious letters started coming for him on a regular basis, and with each one that he opened, Kyros looked paler and more miserable. 'I'm going to die,' he wailed. 'She'll kill me!'

Lana realized that Kyros hadn't been lying when he had told her about Medusa. She thought of a way to save him. At last, she got an idea.

'Take her with you to Australia,' she said, 'to the place where I was working. And do as I say.'

'Go with a monster to Australia?' Kyros was hysterical. 'Are you mad?'

'Well, if she's going to kill you anyway, it's worth a try,' said Lana.

At last, Kyros agreed. He went to see Medusa. 'How many letters did it take to get some sense into you?' she snarled.

'I have been working on your case,' said Kyros, mustering all the courage he had, 'but a problem has cropped up.'

'What?' asked Medusa.

'There's another set of monsters, also called Medusa, who're terrorizing the world right now,' he said. 'it's difficult to steal away the limelight from them unless you eliminate them yourself.'

'Imposters! Who can surpass me? Impossible!'

'Come with me and I'll show you myself,' said Kyros. Using Medusa's magic, Kyros managed to reach the Australian shores with her easily. He pointed at the ocean. 'They inhabit these waters,' he said. 'Look!'

Millions of tiny creatures, with an umbrella-shaped body and several long, hanging tentacles, were swimming about in the ocean, each one looking like a miniature Medusa head. Unknown to Medusa, they were the Irukandji jellyfish, the most venomous jellyfish in the world.

'What? These tiny creatures? See how I destroy them now!' Medusa waded into the waters, right into the midst of all the jellyfish. But her 'gaze that could turn humans to stone' didn't seem to work on the jellyfish, which didn't have eyes! Instead, their tentacles started stinging her.

'Aaaaaah! Help!' cried out the monster, who was slowly being stung to death.

Kyros closed his eyes and turned away. He silently thanked Lana for her presence of mind. He hadn't got any money, but at least he was alive!

Are jellyfish really so dangerous?

Yes, they are!

The Irukandji jellyfish are a group of five species of the smallest but most venomous box jellyfish in the world, of which the main two species are *Carukia barnesi* and

Malo kingi. Found mostly in Australia's oceans, these are named after the Irukandji people who live along the coast north of Queensland. These and many other jellyfish are often commonly called Medusa jellyfish for their dome-shaped body with trailing tentacles, which look similar to the head of 'Medusa,' a monster in Greek mythology.

The Irukandji jellyfish are tiny (about 5–25 mm in length), but when they fire their stingers into their victim, it causes a range of symptoms collectively known as the Irukandji Syndrome. Most jellyfish have stingers only on their tentacles, but the Irukandji also has stingers on its bell. Its stings are so severe that, apart from excruciating pain, they can cause fatal brain haemorrhage.

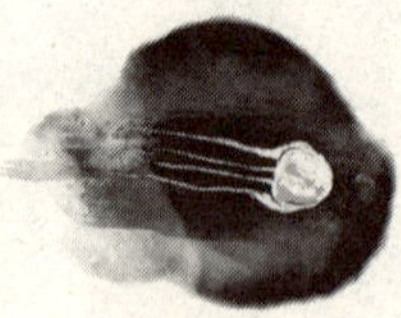

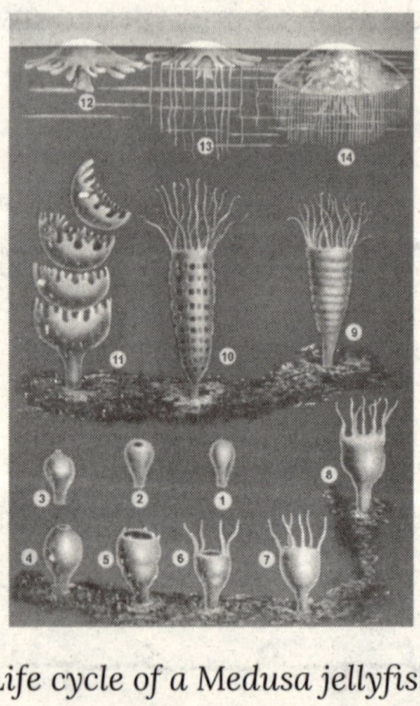

Life cycle of a Medusa jellyfish

14

THE HOARDER AND THE BOARDER

'Not again!' groaned Jimmy, the huge octopus, as his brother Tim came walking nimbly on his eight legs, carrying what looked like a coconut shell. 'Tim, what am I going to do with you?'

Tim, who was much smaller in build, grinned slowly, deftly balancing the shell on top of many others he had brought in. 'Why, what's wrong?' he said, a trifle indignant, but mostly amused at Jimmy's irritation.

'What's *wrong*? Look at all this junk!' exploded Jimmy, while waving his eight arms in eight different directions, trying to emphasize how bad the situation was. 'Your entire home is littered with all sorts of crazy stuff! Stuff that no fish use! The entire ocean is already laughing at you.'

Sure enough, Tim's lair was a wonderland of sorts compared to the otherwise plain, dull homes of the underwater creatures. There were bottle caps and shoes, which people had thrown into the sea at some point of time; jars (some of them with lids), plates and spoons that Tim had salvaged from a shipwreck; rotting photo frames, tiny boxes and chains with pendants that unlucky people had held close to their hearts as they drowned in the ocean's vast depths. A line of coconut shells too adorned the outside of the home now. Tim, however, didn't consider it hoarding; he called it his 'collection of designer items'.

'That's not rubbish,' replied Tim defiantly. 'And if the other creatures don't use this stuff, it's because they don't know *how* to. And there's no use teaching them either; they don't learn.'

'Excuse me?' Jimmy did a double-take. 'You actually tried teaching someone how to "use" this garbage?'

'Well, of course I did,' said Tim, in a hurt voice. 'I was so tired of having this silly multicoloured fish – dunno his name – comment on me all the time that I caught hold of him and tried to put some sense into his head. But, unfortunately, by the end of the lesson, I simply ate him up.'

Jimmy was not at all happy. 'You're supposed to hunt properly; rather, trap your prey using your octopean skills – like camouflage,' he said icily. 'Not pretend to be a teacher and then gobble up your students.'

Tim was hardly bothered. 'Camouflage is just like pretending,' he said, shrugging. 'My tool-wielding skills are way better than your gym-toned, big-muscled arms!'

Gym and exercise were a touchy point for Jimmy. Though he wasn't a hoarder like Tim and usually kept his home spic and span, he had his own obsessions, and one of them happened to be working out at the gym to build his muscles.

'My muscles are definitely going to come in useful someday, unlike your junk,' sneered Jimmy.

'Ha! We'll see about that,' said Tim, snorting. 'One day, you'll be thankful for my junk.'

Though arguments and disagreements were common between the octopus brothers, they loved each other dearly, and one couldn't bear to see the other hurt or upset.

So, when one day, Jimmy returned from his gym session as usual, he was surprised to find Tim's lair empty. Where could he have gone? Jimmy was worried sick.

'Tim, where are you?' he called out, listening in vain for an answer. But none came. He went around the place, sorting out this and that, thinking that Tim must have fallen asleep under a piece of his own junk. But Tim was nowhere to be found!

Jimmy panicked and searched all over. At last, tired, he leant over one of Tim's jars.

Suddenly a tap came from inside the jar. 'Psstt!' came a whisper. 'Have they gone ?'

Startled, Jimmy stared down at the old jar. The lid was slowly turning open! Someone seemed to be turning it from within. An arm poked out. Jimmy caught hold of it and pulled. And tumbling out came Tim!

Tim looked all around with fearful glances, hardly noticing Jimmy. 'Who are you talking about?' cried Jimmy. 'Do you know how long I looked for you? And here you are, playing hide-and-seek and talking all sorts of gibberish!'

'There were humans here,' said Tim, in a scared voice. 'They came after me. I heard one of them saying he wants to cook me and eat me up!'

'And you hid here like a coward?' boomed Jimmy, annoyed. 'Have you forgotten your wonderful gifts? You're an octopus, and well equipped enough to get the better of a hundred humans at once!'

'They were really frightening,' said Tim in a small voice, trembling all over, but wishing he had shown more nerve.

'All right, don't worry, little brother,' said Jimmy, drawing himself up to his full size. 'I'll take care of them.'

'Shall I come with you?' asked Tim eagerly.

'I'll handle it myself,' announced Jimmy. 'But I'm glad you're fine, Tim,' he said, softening a bit. 'I'm glad you hoarded all this. This junk saved your life.'

***

Jimmy set out. After enquiring from a few fishes about which way the humans had gone, he realized that they had dived down from a small fishing boat. He slowly swam up, inspecting the area all around the boat. It looked like they had dropped anchor and the men were relaxing.

'We got a good catch,' Jimmy overheard one saying.

'Pity we couldn't catch the octopus,' said another, who was standing very close to the deck's railing. 'I know of a delicacy made from octopus meat. We could have had it for dinner!'

Jimmy stayed underwater listening to the chatter above, while getting a good hold at the bottom of the vessel. He stretched his long and heavy arms upwards, until they reached the edge of the deck.

Muscular and flexible that he was, Jimmy slowly encircled one of his tentacles around the leg of the man who had been talking. The men seemed unaware of Jimmy's presence and continued their conversation. Suddenly, Jimmy gave a sharp pull. With a startled cry, the man went overboard.

Before the rest of the men could understand what was happening, Jimmy had got almost all his arms around the deck and was using his entire weight to capsize the boat, trying to pull them down towards the ocean depths. The men, screaming and flailing, tried to hold on to the deck railing as the small vessel shook dangerously. A few of them lost balance and fell into the water.

Then, letting go of the vessel, Jimmy used some of his arms to squeeze the rest of the men who were lying on the deck. The men could hardly breathe, so tight was Jimmy's hold on them. Jimmy had no intention of killing them, but he definitely intended to give them the fright of their life. They struggled, gasping for air. Finally, Jimmy let go as he slid back into the water. The men who had fallen in the water had swum to a safe distance and watched fearfully as they saw the beast smoothly swim away from them.

The only man who had not been on the deck till then came running with a gun in his hands. 'What was that creature?' he screamed. 'Whatever it is, it won't escape these bullets!' He peered into the water and took aim, hoping to get rid of the 'monstrous creature'.

But he could no longer see anything in the water! A thick, bluish-black cloud seemed to be spreading in the water around their ship.

'Octopus ink,' he muttered angrily, and started helping his comrades get back on their feet. The group did not stay there a minute longer. 'Not safe to fish in these waters,' declared one, and they beat a hasty retreat to the shore.

Jimmy swam back to Tim, who had been watching the show from below. 'Well? What do you think of my muscles now?' asked Jimmy, proudly.

'Well, I'm glad I didn't spend my time building my own muscles – my brother's got enough for the both of us!' said Tim, laughing away.

Do octopuses really possess so many skills?

Yes, they do!

Octopuses are underwater sea creatures with eight arms, three hearts and beak-like jaws. They are highly intelligent animals, with a long list of defence mechanisms and tactics that they use to survive in the sea. Octopuses learn easily, including learning by observing another octopus. They are also known to be adept at using 'tools', just like humans, such as removing a plug or unscrewing a lid to get prey from a container. A recent discovery showed that octopuses collect coconut shells and use two halves to shelter themselves inside.

Common octopuses collect shells and other objects to construct fortresses, or 'gardens', around their lairs or dens. They use camouflage to escape detection, by changing the pigment that colours their skin cells. However, if they're discovered, they release a spray of bluish-black ink to confuse their enemies, and make an escape. The ink also contains a substance that dulls a predator's sense of smell, making the fleeing octopus harder to track. All octopuses are venomous, but only the bite of the small blue-ringed octopus is known to be lethal to humans.

They are fast swimmers and can squeeze into the smallest of cracks and crevices where predators can't get at them. If all its defences fail, an octopus can lose an arm to escape a predator's grasp and regenerate it later.

15

THE LURE OF THE LIGHT

Mr Shrimp was unhappy. He wandered through the ocean waters, trying to find the meaning of life. His friends had ditched him, his family had disowned him, and now he was all alone. He was very, very sad. He swam on slowly, kicking at empty shells and wondering how he could do better.

He stopped by a reef, where he could see the fish and other sea creatures having a gala time. He peeped from the outside, but dared not join them. He was such a loser! The fish would all either make fun of him or pity him. He could never be one of them. He was just about to continue his aimless roaming when he saw a poster put up on one of the corals.

Upset with life? Do not lose hope, for your saviour is here! Find peace and happiness in believing in the

Light! Let the Light guide you! Strengthen your belief, you common sea creature, and come into the Light!

A picture of an oval ball of glowing light was crudely drawn below these words, and an address mentioned underneath. Mr Shrimp's face lit up. *I might be able to get some guidance after all*, he thought joyfully. The address directed him right into the dark depths of the ocean, sinister and dangerous.

Ah, well, never mind, he thought to himself. *The greatest of seers do not mingle with the common fish in the packed shallow waters.*

He immediately set out.

The shrimp swam on and on, till the waters around him became darker and darker. He was just beginning to lose hope when he saw a flickering light.

'Ah, there's the light! I see it!' Mr Shrimp cried and swam on bravely. The light swayed to and fro, shining brightly like a ray of hope. The light seemed to be calling out to him and he swam to it as if in a daze.

'The light will save me,' he muttered senselessly, and swam on.

***

Nobody knew what became of Mr Shrimp.

Rumours erupted all around. Some said he had got caught in a fishing net. Others said he had swum to warmer waters to start a new life. Some, who claimed to have seen him swim towards the depths, said he had received enlightenment from a strange divine source and had become unrecognizable, but still swam freely among them as a new fish.

Mr Herring was the next one to receive enlightenment. He had hurt his tail fin while trying to escape a sea lion, and not a single day passed without worry. Then one day, he heard of the mysterious divine presence that offered solace to troubled souls. *I must try to find it*, he thought to himself.

He thought of telling his other fish friends first, but then thought better of it. *I better receive the blessings first myself*, he thought, and went off in search of the light. As he entered the heart of the ocean, he spotted it. It seemed to be calling out to him. 'Come into the light,' it seemed to say. 'Experience the peace...'

Mr Herring, as if in a trance, dumbly followed the light.

Two days later, hysterical weeping could be heard from Mr Herring's house. 'Herring is nowehere to be found,' Mrs Herring wailed.

The fish who heard her wails couldn't figure out if Mr Herring was dead, or alive but elsewhere.

However, soon, the hue and cry died down.

Then one day, two little tuna fish decided to go in search of the light. 'I heard you get divine powers and the blessings will be enough to let us write our exams without studying,' said Mydion, the first tuna, happily. Mydion did very badly at school. The other tuna, Lily, however, was a good student and was quite sceptical of Mydion's idea. 'I don't think that can help us. We will still have to study...'

'Oh, come on, Lily, let's just go and pray to the Light,' said Mydion. 'Just think how much trouble it will save us! I really think it might work.'

The two young fish made their way to the ocean deep. Just like Mr Shrimp and Mr Herring before them, they found the strange light, floating away from them, deeper and deeper, but beckoning to them all the same. Both Mydion and Lily were entranced. They swam faster and faster.

'I'll get my blessings first,' cried Mydion.

'No, I shall,' cried Lily.

They raced ahead, trying to outdo each other to get to the Light first. The Light was becoming bigger and bigger. They were almost near it.

'I'll get the Light's blessings first,' cried Lily as she almost reached it.

'Oh no, you won't!' Mydion shoved her out of the way, and both fishes tumbled out of the path, landing a few feet away from the 'light'.

And that was when the two fish snapped back to their senses.

Right above the 'light' was a creature waiting to devour them, its jaws wide open! The 'light', in fact, was a bulb attached to the creature's chin. It could produce its own light! They could hardly see the form of the creature, for its body was pitch black, thin and long. But fearsome were its teeth, long and sharp. The creature seemed annoyed that its meal hadn't gone straight into its open mouth as on the previous occasions. It writhed and wriggled in anger, and its long, snake-like body lit up, all along the front and the back, showing its real form!

'Oh, no! This is the black dragonfish!' cried out Lily, who had heard of it. 'Let's get out of here!'

Mydion didn't wait to respond. Both fish swam away hurriedly, but the dragonfish gave chase!

'How can it see us and hunt us?' cried Mydion. 'It's so dark here!'

'She emits her own light that we can't see!' said Lily. 'We can only see that bulb under her chin!'

'She? How do you know it's a female?' cried Mydion again, mystified.

'The male dragonfish can't feed,' cried Lily in reply, all the while trying to swim furiously away. 'They're small and weak!'

The dragonfish was still hot on their trail and the two little fish were getting tired from the chase.

'Why can't she let us go?' wailed Mydion. 'We are just two tiny little fish! She must be getting so many other prey!'

'She must be really hungry!' said Lily, struggling to catch her breath. 'Like Shakespeare said, the ...'

Is this the time to discuss English literature?' retorted a panicky Mydion. 'Can't we just flee?'

Despite the bickering, at last the two fish escaped to the shallower, brighter waters of the ocean, leaving the dragonfish far behind. They had had a lucky escape, and Mydion decided that studying hard was far better than the promise of quick remedies and hallucinating lights. Lily was only too happy to help him out with the English literature part.

Does the dragonfish really exist?

Yes, it does!

The black dragonfish (*Idiacanthus atlanticus*) is found in the waters of the subtropical oceans closer to the Antarctic at almost 5000–6000 feet below the surface of the sea. It belongs to *Stomiidae*, a family of deep-sea ray-finned fish. The male and the female of the species are vastly different in their appearance, feeding habits and lifespan. The female black dragons are about 2 feet (61 cm) long and have fang-like teeth and a long chin whisker (the light-producing or bio-luminescent 'barbel'). But the males are small, about 3 inches (8 cm) in length, and brownish in colour, and have no teeth, chin barbel or stomach. Unable to eat, the male lives only long enough to mate.

The females attract prey to their teeth-filled mouths using the bio-luminescent barbel that hangs from its chin. As they are 'ambush predators,' their bodies are dark black, and even their stomachs are coated with black tissue to block out any light that might be produced by bio-luminescent animals that they eat. The female dragonfish is covered with photophores (specialized light cells) along its lower and upper surfaces, and has photophores under its eyes and at the end of its long barbel. When disturbed, it lights up all over, even down the lengths of its fins. Through its photophores (except those under its eyes), it produces blue-green light – the wavelengths that travel farthest in the ocean, thus attracting prey from afar. However, the photophores under its eyes emit a red light. This red light illuminates the unsuspecting prey, thus letting the dragonfish see in the dark.

16

GLOWING IN THE DARK, DYING IN THE LIGHT

Jane was impressed by all the hustle and bustle around her. New Jersey seemed a wonderful place to live and work, a far cry from her country home in Nevada, where only the mines offered abundant employment. It was the year 1919, and the First World War had just ended. While the rest of the world was reeling under the effects of the war, America was far from it. America's industries and factories were safe – demand had increased greatly, and so had production. Business seemed to be booming, and she could see busy shops and factories everywhere, and workers hurrying to their place of work. It definitely looked like she would find a good job in New Jersey.

'How long will you gape open-mouthed, Jane?' asked Katherine, Jane's friend, who had brought her there. 'This is just the town of Orange. What will you say when you see the entire state?'

Jane was too tongue-tied with awe to reply immediately. 'I say, Kat, this is a swell place. I'm beginning to believe there are good times ahead for us.'

'Well, of course there are,' replied Kat confidently. 'Come along now, or I'll be late too.'

Kat hurried along, taking long strides. *She walks in style*, thought Jane, glancing down at her own plain appearance. Kat looked every bit the modern woman in her checked shirt and trousers, with a red scarf at her throat, and her face made up with blush and lipstick. Jane felt quite conscious in her drab grey dress that almost came down to her ankles.

'Exactly what am I supposed to do at this factory where you work?' Jane asked breathlessly, struggling to keep up with Kat. She worked at the United States Radium Corporation.

'Oh, it's easy enough,' said Kat. 'All you need to do is paint the watch dials with the glow-in-the-dark paint they give you. It's the in thing now, you know, glow-in-the-dark watches.'

Jane was stupefied. 'And they pay 8 cents apiece for this? Is that all I need to do?' Jane couldn't believe it. It was very good money, for such a simple job.

'That's all,' answered Kat. 'And we paint up to 300 watches every day. So you can imagine how good it is.'

Jane looked around her and found that what Kat said was true. Radium, or the metal that made stuff glow in the dark, seemed to be everywhere. While one sign said, 'Radium watches, so you can outshine time,' another said, 'Radithor – the radium drink: to get back your youthful energy!' A pharmacy had a banner outside proclaiming the great qualities of Radione, 'the wonder drug that gives ordinary water life-giving properties'.

***

Jane quietly followed Kat into the factory, where she met some of Kat's friends who worked there too. 'You can watch us at work today – see how simple it will be,' they assured her.

Jane sat down at an adjoining table, while Kat took her place on the assembly line along with the other girls. There was a huge can of radium paint there, which they used to paint the watch dials with. They laughed and talked as they worked, and Jane started to feel that it was the best thing to do in the world for a poor, uneducated girl like her.

'This is really a nice job,' she said, as she came to know the others better. 'And being with you all makes it feel like heaven.'

'Oh, it's nice and easy alright,' said Grace, another worker there, as she carefully painted a 6 on the watch dial, licking the paintbrush at intervals to get a sharp pointy end.

'But if I smudge the numbers, I might get a good licking from old Smith, our supervisor – which is why

I have to lick the brush!' she joked, while the others laughed along.

'Is Mr Smith that bad?' asked Jane, a bit apprehensive.

'Nah, he isn't – he just can't stand sloppiness or bad work,' said Edna, another friend of Kat's. 'So he'll shout his head off and threaten to fire you, but nothing more than that.'

'I'll speak to Mr Smith about the job in the evening,' thought Jane.

As the girls worked, a few people passed their room, wearing whitish-silver coats and helmet-like headgear. 'Who are they?' asked Jane, puzzled by their outfit.

The other girls giggled. 'Scientists, they say,' chuckled one. 'Working hard day and night. And what do they invent? Glow-in-the-dark paint!' Peals of laughter followed.

Hmm...why were they wearing such protective gear, thought Jane. But she was soon distracted by the lively discussions among the girls.

'We use this paint to paint our nails too,' said one.

'I once painted my teeth with it,' said another. 'What a scare I gave my landlady when I smiled at her in the dark!'

Just then, Mr Smith walked in. Jane stood up in a hurry, all flustered. But unfortunately, she knocked off the can of paint that was on the table.

'How dare you?' screamed Mr Smith. 'Who even let you inside? Out! Out this minute!'

Jane hurried outside, not having the courage to explain or argue.

That evening, she waited outside till Kat came out.

'He'll never give me a job now,' she wailed. 'I suppose I better look for a job elsewhere.'

'I'm afraid you'll have to do that, Jane,' said Kat, who had tried reasoning with Smith, and failed.

So Jane was on her own again. She went from factory to factory, and at last found a place in a cloth-dyeing factory.

***

A couple of years passed. Jane was surprised to get a letter one day from Grace. 'Katherine is dying,' it said. 'Come and visit her while you still can.'

Horrified, Jane rushed to the apartment where the girls had been staying. She was shocked to find her stylish friend Kat in a way she couldn't even imagine – her jaw was almost eaten away! The other girls all looked sick and haggard as well. Whatever had happened?

'One of the girls died at the factory,' said Grace. 'We were all sick too – and we found it was due to radium poisoning. But I suppose it's too late now.' She sighed.

'But you can't let the factory off like that! Did they tell you that the paint was poisonous?'

'They didn't,' said Edna. 'Our hands started to glow in the dark first. We thought it was just the powder on the skin. Abigail – her bones crumbled and disintegrated...' Edna broke down.

'But what you said is right, Jane,' said Grace suddenly, 'we must fight for justice.'

And then started a long-drawn-out legal fight with the factory, with Grace at the head of it. Jane tried her best to be there for the girls, but the poisoning was too strong. They won the case, but suffered too much, too soon. Jane couldn't forget the day she had dropped the can of paint; the mistake had saved her from a speedy burial in a lead-lined coffin.

Did the 'Radium Girls' really exist?

Yes, they did.

Marie and Pierre Curie, Polish and French chemists, discovered radium in 1898, which won them the Nobel Prize, but cost them their lives. Radium is a highly radioactive element and can be extremely dangerous. But in the early years of its discovery, it was used in several products, including wristwatches and toothpaste, and thought to have healing properties – that was, until its intense radioactivity began to have terrible effects on people's health.

The Radium Girls were female factory workers who were employed at the United States Radium factory in Orange, New Jersey, USA, sometime around 1917, to paint watch dials with luminous paint. Since the paint contained radium, they suffered from the deadly effects of radiation. Sadly, they had been told that the paint was harmless, and they ended up consuming deadly amounts of radium by licking their paintbrushes to give them a fine point. Some also painted their fingernails, face and teeth with the glowing substance.

A dial painter could paint up to 300 dials daily, earning as much as US $24 a day. But the worker would end up licking her brush for a fine point up to 15 times per dial – meaning that she could consume around 4,000 micrograms of radium in six months – an amount thousand times deadlier than the smallest dose that is required to kill a person.

In the 1920s, several dial painters complained of ill health, and their symptoms were slowly linked to their work with radium. The women suffered from advanced radiation sickness with symptoms ranging from anaemia to the horrifying disintegration of the jawbone, which came to be known as 'radium jaw'. When they died, they had to be placed in lead-lined coffins to absorb the intense radiation emanating from their corpses.

Plant worker Grace Fryer sued the company along with five others, and the lawsuit became an important milestone for health and labour rights.

17

THE ROOSTER'S SCARY ANCESTOR

Kenny the cat eyed the chicken coop in the backyard from the third floor. He was seated on the windowsill of the children's bedroom, shared by the Finnigan kids, Scarlet and Thomas. With a golden bell tied around his neck, he was sure he looked utterly stupid. He did not venture out into the alley anymore, because he was scared of what the other cats would think of him. The bell had been Scarlet's idea; she thought he looked cute. Thomas had wrinkled his nose at the notion, and Mrs Finnigan had suggested a simple bow tie. But Scarlet would have none of it; Kenny was, after all, *her* pet.

Kenny lazily got up and stretched. It looked like the help hadn't let the chickens out today. The fat Bantam hen had laid a brood of eggs a month ago and had clucked away in delight. Kenny had been waiting impatiently since then for the chicks to arrive. But from the time the eggs had hatched, the chicks were never left alone; either they fussed around the mother hen or the tall, frowning rooster stood in the vicinity, looking darkly at everyone and everything that passed by. Oh, how Kenny wanted to eat those chicks! Birds were meant to be eaten by cats, according to Kenny.

He, however, hadn't tried catching the bustling fat hen or the tall scarecrow-like Bantam rooster. They were too much trouble and probably wouldn't taste as good – the meat must be hard to chew, was the reason he gave his friends in the alley. The street cats nudged each other whenever Kenny said this.

'A case of sour grapes,' they whispered to each other.

'He doesn't have the guts,' said one.

'The rooster is taller than him,' said another. 'The hen would peck him to death.'

Then one day, Kenny heard them. 'Neither am I scared of them, nor are they bigger than me,' he said angrily, 'They are just silly, weak birds, and they have always been so!' He got into a fight with the cats who had teased him. After a great deal of biting and scratching, he had turned up at the doorstep of the Finnigan household, a complete mess.

This was what had led to the bell around his neck, for Scarlet thought she could catch him if he tried to go away again. Now as he yawned and meowed, the bell under his neck jingled a bit. Seated in her armchair, trying out needlework, Scarlet started and looked up. 'Don't move, Kitty,' she said. 'I'm warning you.'

Thomas, her older brother, was in bed with a cold and cough. 'Oh, give it a rest, Scarlet,' he groaned. 'Let the cat go where it wants. What with you and your warnings, and the cat's bell ringing all the time, I simply cannot sleep.'

'Well, he's my cat, and I can't let him get hurt again, can I?' asked Scarlet obstinately. Thomas gave up trying to sleep. He picked up his book on dinosaurs and started reading it.

Kenny sat down again, keenly watching the goings-on in the yard. It looked like the chicks were about to be let out. He sat up with a start when the little chicks came running out - plump and fluffy little yellow balls that looked like dots from the third-floor window. The bell around his neck rang madly, giving away his excitement.

Scarlet picked him up from the windowsill. 'Trying to get away to the alley again?' she said, putting him in her lap. 'Bad kitty, bad kitty!' she scolded. Little did Scarlet know that all he wanted to do was eat the little chicks.

Thomas looked up from his book. 'For heaven's sake, stop cuddling that cat as if it were a kitten,' said Thomas. 'It's probably got fleas from those other cats. And its name is Kenny, not Kitty.'

Kenny scowled as a cat would scowl, his hair rising up and his whiskers twitching. *Fleas? How could Thomas say that he had those pesky things?*

'Well, I will call him Kitty, because it sounds nicer,' said Scarlet.

She kept patting Kenny while he squirmed and fidgeted, wanting to get out in the yard and have a go at those chicks.

Just then, Scarlet's mother called out for her. 'Coming, Mother!' she answered, and deposited Kenny right beside Thomas. 'Make sure he doesn't get away,' she said. 'I'll be right back!'

Thomas kept a hand on Kenny and continued reading his book. Kenny didn't mind Thomas so much, because he didn't pat him or fuss over him the way Scarlet did. But today he wanted to get away to the yard. He peeped into the book and saw a picture of a giant, scary-looking angry bird, which he didn't recognize; its eyes seemed hypnotic and frightening, watching him out of the book. At the bottom of the page was another picture – of a weak-looking common fowl, just like the Bantam rooster in the yard.

'Do you know what this book says, Kenny?' asked Thomas. 'It says that this large bird here –the Archaeopteryx – was actually a bird-like dinosaur and the ancestor of our common chickens.'

Kenny growled in disbelief. What! Such a terrifying ancestor for those silly birds?

'And look at all these dinosaurs here,' Thomas turned the pages of the book. 'But the chickens aren't so scary, are they?' he asked the cat good-humouredly. Kenny purred in reply.

'I'll have my cough syrup now and try to sleep for a while,' said Thomas absent-mindedly to Kenny. 'Now be a good cat.'

Thomas took a spoonful of syrup and put the bottle back on the table, but forgot to screw back the lid. He lay back. The syrup was making him feel drowsy, and Thomas closed his eyes.

Kenny stealthily moved out, trying not to make much noise with his bell. But as he moved across the table, the bottle tipped over and the floor was covered with a milky-white liquid.

'Is this milk?' wondered Kenny. 'Might be a good appetizer before I eat the chicken,' he thought and lapped up some of it. It tasted horrible, though.

Kenny slunk away, all the way down to the yard. He was feeling more and more confident now, with neither the help nor the hen nor the rooster in sight. He could hear the chicks chirping away, and he moved ahead, towards a particularly plump little one.

Something was wrong...

Kenny felt dazed. It seemed like there wasn't one chicken but two!

The chick suddenly seemed double in front of his eyes. *Ah well, the more the better*, he thought and moved on, though his eyes were losing focus. When he thought he was close by, he pounced. 'Caught you!' he cried. But when he looked, it was no longer a little yellow chick in front of him. It was that large,

dinosaur-like bird with the nasty glistening eyes that stood in front of him, towering over him. 'How dare you attack my little ones?' came a booming voice. That was the last thing that Kenny heard, as he trembled in fright and fainted.

When Kenny came to, he found himself back in the third-floor bedroom, in Scarlet's lap. 'Poor thing, we found him lying asleep in the yard with the rooster madly pecking at him,' Scarlet was saying. 'Thomas, I told you to take care of him!'

'How did I know he would drink my cough syrup?' asked Thomas indignantly. 'Well, there's nothing wrong with him. The rooster gave him a fright, that's all.'

No, *you silly child, it was not the rooster, it was that humungous bird from your horrible book*, Kenny wanted to say, but all he could do was hiss and fret and scratch at Scarlet's frock.

'Calm down, Kitty,' scolded Scarlet. 'Bad kitty, bad kitty!'

Are the common fowl and dinosaurs related?

Yes, they are!

For decades, palaeontologists have been trying to understand how reptiles and birds are related – the only answer, so far, is an extinct bird. A 'hybrid' creature with feathered wings, but with the teeth and long bony tail of a dinosaur, the Archaeopteryx is considered the missing evolutionary link between birds and reptiles.

The Archaeopteryx is said to be the first bird that lived 150 million years ago, and the ancestor of modern-day birds. It is an evolutionary form between flying birds and non-avian (that means 'not birds') feathered dinosaurs like Compsognathus and predatory dinosaurs like Deinonichus. In fact, it is said that modern birds, and even the common chicken, has evolved ultimately from the famous *Tyrannosaurus rex*. By analysing the proteins found in a *T. rex* fossil, scientists have placed the Archaeopteryx on the evolutionary tree between alligators, and chickens and ostriches.

While originally a reptile, the Archaeopteryx appears to have acquired its bird-like features – feathers, wings and flight – in just 10 million years. The Archaeopteryx had a full set of teeth, a flat chest bone, a long bony tail, gastralia ('belly ribs') and three claws on the wing that could have been used to grasp prey (or perhaps trees). However, its feathers, wings, furcula ('wishbone') and reduced fingers are all similar to the features found in the birds of today.

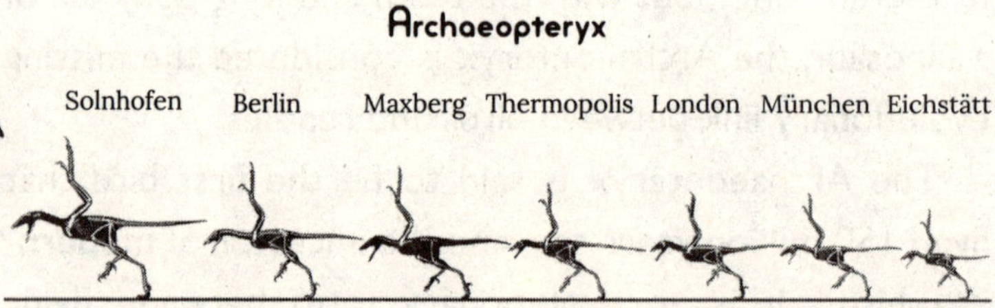

Scientists have restored the skeletal remains of various Archaeopteryx found in different places to get an idea of what they looked like

18

WHAT MUMMY WISHED FOR

Akhila's mother, Saritha, frowned at the report in her hand. Her younger brother, Akash, peeped out from behind the curtains of his room to watch the scene. After Akhila, it would be his turn to show his report card.

'Hmm,' a sound escaped Saritha's lips. 'not as bad as I thought it would be,' she said, finally. 'Thankfully, you have managed to score 85 per cent, despite your illness. So what does this prove?'

Akhila gulped. Was that praise or blame? She said nothing and nervously pushed up her glasses on the bridge of her nose.

Saritha looked up, a little irritated. 'It proves that you can do much better,' she said. 'If you could score 85 per cent even though you were sick, it shows that you can score 95 per cent or even more when you are completely fine. And this means you haven't been working enough to do the best you can. Why have you never been able to cross 90 per cent? Why couldn't you score better in mathematics? Don't we send you for tuition? How is it that the others can score and you...'

The scolding went on for a while, and Akhila silently listened to it all. Her mind wandered to dwell on the new cartoon series that would begin that weekend. However, her mother's sharp tone brought her back to the present.

'Speak up!' Saritha demanded. 'How much did Sandhya score?'

'Sandhya...she got 90 per cent,' lied Akhila. Actually Sandhya, her classmate and also her neighbour, had scored 94 per cent, but Akhila knew that the truth would get her another earful.

'You better make up for this in the final exams,' said Saritha sternly before letting her daughter off.

Poor Akash, however, had not scored even 80 per cent in that unit test, nor did he have the excuse of having been sick. Seeing his mother scold Akhila, he decided to give her the slip. He quickly fed the turtles in his large aquarium some food. 'Here's your quota for the day,' he said. 'Don't expect me back until dark!'

The six turtles looked up at the food and at him in a disinterested sort of way and went about their slow, lazy life again. Akash jumped out of the window into the garden and ran out to join his friends in the park. But he left the report card on his table, so that Saritha would see it when he was out.

Saritha was fuming at Akash's report card when her neighbour, Sandhya's mother, walked in. 'Saritha, I heard Akhila fared badly because of her illness,' she said cheerfully. 'Sandhya got 96 per cent.' (This too was a lie.) Saritha vowed she would ensure that Akhila and Akash secured the first place in the final exams.

***

Unknown to the mothers who were preparing their children for a battle for marks, a different but equally tough clash was happening in Akash's glass tank that housed the turtles. Three female turtles were about to lay eggs, and the soon-to-be mothers were already

making claims. The three females, who had been named 'Un, Dos, Tres' by a Spanish-obsessed Akash, were already talking about their unborn offspring.

Un had taken up residence in the sand just below the incandescent bulb and intended to lay her eggs there. 'It's warm here, and I will have beautiful girls come out of my eggs,' she declared.

Tres, on the other hand, had taken up a spot close to the window. 'The cool night breeze is definitely going to give me handsome male offspring,' she said.

Only Dos was left without a spot. She hadn't known the dynamics of child rearing, having been brought up in captivity herself. She innocently asked Un how she knew she was going to have female babies. 'Oh, don't you know? If the temperature's higher around the eggs, they'll become females,' she said. 'And this bulb makes the water really warm just here.'

'And if the temperature's cool, you get male babies,' Tres chimed in.

Dos was confused. She wanted both male and female babies! But both Un and Tres spoke as though one was superior to the other. She decided to divide up her eggs between the two spots. But neither of the other two would hear of it!

'No way!' said Un, drawing a line in the sand around the area lit up by the bulb. 'I found this spot first, and it's reserved for my eggs.'

'Can't help, I need this spot for my brood,' said Tres, clutching her eggs, when Dos asked her to move a little and make place for her.

In the end, poor Dos had to lay her eggs in the sand midway between the bulb and the window, under a decorative coral. As the expectant mothers ticked off the days from the calendar to welcome their babies, Akhila's and Sandhya's mothers ticked off the days to the annual exams and the announcement of results.

It was the competition between the human mothers that turned the tables for the turtles. As Saritha pushed and prodded her children to study harder, Sandhya's mother did the same. Both sent the children for extra tuitions and classes, and poor Akash had no time to pay attention to his water tank and pet turtles, except to give them food.

Unfortunately for Un, the incandescent bulb blew out and stopped working, and Akash didn't get the time to replace it. Saritha made sure that the windows in Akash's room stayed closed during the night, to ensure that he didn't catch a cold during the exams. While Un's spot became quite cool, Tres's spot became unbearably warm, much to the chagrin of the two!

When D-day arrived, everyone was anxious with expectation. Saritha found that both Akash and Akhila had managed to score 95 per cent in their exams! She rejoiced.

Akash was finally relieved, and walked in on his beloved tortoises to find that their eggs had all hatched. Un was, however, looking sad; she had got all male babies, thanks to the burnt-out bulb. Tres was grumpily watching her female babies wander around in the water. Only Dos, who had found the middle spot, was truly happy. She had got a mixed brood of male and female babies!

Can temperature decide the gender in marine creatures?

Yes, it can, and does!

While humans and most mammals, birds and insects have their gender determined by the chromosomes they inherit from their parents, some fish and a few reptiles like alligators and turtles experience what is known as temperature-dependent sex determination (TSD), where the temperature around the developing eggs determines the offsping's gender.

For instance, in many turtle species, lower temperatures cause eggs to hatch as all males, and eggs from warmer nests turn out to be all females. If a turtle's eggs are incubated below 27.7° C, the turtle hatchlings will be male. If the eggs incubate above 31°C, the hatchlings will be female. Temperatures that fluctuate between the two extremes will produce a mix of male and female baby turtles.

Other cases show the reverse. For example, when it comes to the American alligator's eggs, incubation at higher temperatures such as 33°C produces mostly males, while incubation at lower temperatures of 30°C produces mostly females. A joint team of Japanese and US researchers has determined that the thermo-sensor protein TRPV4 is associated with TSD in the American alligator.

How is climate change related to this phenomenon? As the earth becomes warmer due to geological or man-made activity, TSD may give rise to only males or only females, depending on the species, causing a skewed sex ratio (the number of males and females in a population). This can mean fewer offspring, which, over time, leads to complete extinction.

19

THE LIVING DRAGON WITHIN

It had been a long hike through the forests of Ghana for Kojo and his younger brother Kofi, and they were very hungry, thirsty and tired.

Their father was the present chief of their tribe. Every year, their father, along with another elder of the tribe, or with Kojo, made this journey to meet the chief of the neighbouring tribe, to offer him gifts as a symbol of friendship and peace from their own tribe. This year, the two brothers took on this responsibility, especially since Kojo, being the eldest, was expected to become the next chief of their tribe soon.

'When will we be back home?' asked Kofi, bending over to catch his breath. He was not very interested in his tribe's customs and rituals. He had completed his schooling in the city, a rarity among his tribe. He wanted to settle down in a town, though he was careful not to reveal his plans to his father or brothers.

His family, on the other hand, hoped he would follow their way of life even after his education.

This was Kofi's first such journey, an initiation into the tribe's customs, and Kojo hoped that his younger brother had learnt something about maintaining diplomatic relations with other tribes. He smiled indulgently at Kofi's impatience.

The vast grasslands with bunches of shrubs dotting the landscape stretched before them, before converging into a dense forest on the horizon. 'Only half a day more,' he said, walking on. 'Do you want to take a break?'

He didn't hear an answer and turned around to check where Kofi was. Kofi had simply plonked himself on the ground, completely worn out. 'Yes, I need a little rest,' he mouthed. Kojo relented and came back to sit down with Kofi.

They had very little food left with them. Though they had been given enough food for their return journey by the chief whom they had visited, Kofi had left it behind in his excitement to leave. Kojo didn't approve of going back and asking for it – it would hurt the pride of their tribe. So they had trudged on, trying to eat and drink as little as they could, to stretch their supplies.

As Kofi snoozed on Kojo's shoulder, Kojo calculated that they would get home the next day – Friday. Kojo smiled to himself. Kojo and Kofi were named after days of the week. In Ghana, children were named after the day of the week they were born on: '*kojo*' meant 'born on Monday' in their tribe's language and '*kofi*' meant 'born on Friday'. Their first name was followed by their family name.

***

It was almost dusk when Kojo shook Kofi awake. 'Shall we eat?' asked Kofi as soon as he opened his eyes. Kojo unpacked their little cloth bundle to fish out the leftovers of the *kelewele* and yam pottage. They didn't have any water left. Kojo found a pond nearby and led Kofi to it.

The water looked greenish black in the slanting rays of the sun. Was it good enough to drink, wondered Kofi. Kojo shrugged. Children of the forest ate what was available and drank what Nature gave them, he told Kofi. He cupped his hands and drank deeply.

Kofi, however, stood away, still undecided about drinking the water. Kojo did not force him. He drank a few more times. He felt he had swallowed a few insects with the water. But how did that matter? The insects would die in his stomach, he thought. Soon, they resumed their journey and reached home on Friday, as Kojo had figured.

***

Kojo was soon made the chief of his tribe. A year passed by, and everything was well. He was loved by his tribespeople, and his father was proud of him. Kofi, meanwhile, had gone back to the city and enrolled in a university. Kojo and the rest of the family missed him, but they hoped it was all for his good.

Then, one day, Kojo felt something wrong with his leg. There was a painful blister forming on his foot and it bothered him a lot. He tried to remember if he had unknowingly hurt himself in the forest, or if a thorn had lodged itself in his skin. There was no injury that he could remember, but the blister got worse. He tried local remedies, but they were of no use. The herbal pastes did nothing to heal it. Finally, he got a little relief when he dipped his foot in the river close to their village.

Yet he couldn't he keep his foot in the water all day! He had his duties as a chief to attend to; he had his responsibilities as the head of his family too. Crippled by the pain, he limped back each day, after spending some time at the river. He could no longer concentrate on his regular tasks. He could hear people whispering about his inefficiency. Heart-broken, he turned to his father.

'I am too sick to carry on, Father,' he cried from his bed. 'I cannot bear the pitying looks of these very people who once loved and respected me. Is there no cure for this agony, Father?'

'My son, this is a terrible affliction,' said his father, with tears in his eyes. 'I have known many people to have suffered the same way, and some have been through worse. You have been brave to carry on this far. But do not worry. I have sent a message to Kofi. He says he will bring someone to treat you.'

That night, Kofi came with his friend, a doctor from the city. The medic examined Kojo and said, 'There is a worm – called a Guinea worm – living inside your foot. Once it is removed, you will be free from pain.'

Kojo beamed with hope.

'But it may take days, even weeks to remove it,' the doctor continued. 'Are you ready for that?'

Kojo nodded. All he wanted was to get rid of the terrible creature inside him that had made his life a living hell. The doctor immersed Kojo's foot in a tub of cold water. As he watched, the end of a long, white thread-like worm slowly appeared out of the blister. The doctor took a small stick and immediately wound the worm around it, not letting it go back inside the body. Over many days, the doctor wound the worm completely on the stick, little by little, eventually removing it entirely from Kojo's leg.

'Here is the little dragon that bothered you, Chief Kojo,' he said, smiling. 'From now on, remember not to drink stagnant water that contains water fleas!'

Does a 'dragon worm' really exist?

Yes, it does.

Dracunculus medinensis, also called the Guinea worm or the dragon or dragon worm, is a parasite that causes 'Dracunculiasis' – a debilitating condition, where the female adult worm lives and grows inside the human body to a length of 60–100 cm. People become infected with the Guinea worm by drinking water from ponds and other standing water containing tiny 'water fleas' that carry the Guinea worm larvae. The larvae are eaten by the water fleas that live in these water bodies.

Once a person drinks such infected water, the larvae penetrate the digestive track, passing into the body cavity. During the next 10–14 months, the female larvae grow into full-size adults. When the adult female worm is ready to come out, it creates a blister on the skin anywhere on the body, but usually on the legs and feet.

This blister causes a very painful 'burning' feeling and it bursts within 24–72 hours. Immersing the affected body part into water helps relieve the pain. It also causes the Guinea worm to come out of the wound and release a milky white liquid, which contains millions of larvae, into the water. This contaminates the water supply and starts the cycle all over again.

Rod of Asclepius

There is no vaccination for this worm nor a cure for this condition other than to remove the worm by slowly winding it on a long stick, for days together. If one tries to kill the worm by chopping or breaking off its protruding head from the blister, the worm releases high levels of antigens into the bloodstream, leading to the death of the patient.

Though this disease is still seen in areas (especially in areas to the south of the Sahara Desert in Africa) that have poor access to healthcare, there is an organized effort to eradicate the disease by wiping out the parasitic organism – the Guinea worm itself – from the face of the earth: a kind of an effort at man-made extinction.

What's more, the Rod of Asclepius, or the Greek symbol denoting medicine and healing – a staff with a serpent wound around it – is said, by some, to be a depiction of the traditional treatment given to cure the Guinea worm disease.

20

THE TREES HAVE EARS

Andrew sneezed loudly. It did look like he was coming down with a bad cold.

'Shhh!' said William, next to him. 'Keep it down!' he hissed. 'Do you want us to be found out?'

'I can't help it,' Andrew said, his voice hoarse. 'And I'm sure the English aren't around here anywhere. We can safely discuss our plans of ambushing their cavalry at New Park.'

It was the year 1314, and Andrew and William were two Scottish knights who served in the army of King Bruce of Scotland. They were preparing themselves to fend off the English Army led by King Edward II, who was trying to regain his hold over Scotland. But the proud and patriotic Scots were determined to achieve complete freedom for their beloved country, and moreover, they loved their ruler, King Bruce.

'You never know where they plan to attack from,' William said gloomily. 'They have a much stronger army than ours!'

'And that's exactly why I don't think we should be wasting our precious army guarding this silly forest route!' burst out Andrew. 'Why would they take a longer route to Stirling Castle? They could confidently attack us head-on by the regular path!' He finished this statement of his with another violent sneeze.

***

The two of them had been sent to explore the woods to the north and west of the Stirling Castle, to make sure that no Englishmen would try to make their way in from there. King Bruce had taken up his position at New Park along with most of their army. They had laid siege to Stirling Castle, which was the only place that had any followers left who were still faithful to England's King Edward. Now Edward was trying to send in his army to take over Stirling Castle and lift the siege, so that his followers could be freed and the Scots could be defeated.

William looked up at the huge, tall trees that made up the woods. They were dark and deep, and light penetrated only up to a few metres ahead. The rest merged into dark silhouettes in the undergrowth. Vines and creepers grew abundantly, threatening to ensnare gullible travellers. Large, fleshy, brownish fungal structures grew on the trees in abundance. A crossbill cried somewhere, and another bird answered its call. On the whole, it was a very eerie place.

'Even I'm not really convinced that the English might attack from here,' said William slowly, looking around. 'Unless, of course—'

'Unless what?' demanded Andrew.

'Unless they intend to climb up the cliff and get into the castle from behind,' said William.

Stirling Castle was surrounded on three sides by steep cliffs, and the only way in, or out, was through the fourth side. 'Pah!' snorted Andrew. 'Impossible!'

A frightened red fox darted out of the undergrowth as if it were being chased, and gave a quick look of fear at Andrew and William. It then bounded away immediately.

Andrew and William hardly noticed this. They were used to the sights and sounds of the forest. They walked on, Andrew rubbing his nose, and sniffling from time to time.

But, as they walked on, William became slightly wary and hesitant. Suddenly, a twig snapped behind them.

William almost jumped out of his skin. Andrew cleared his throat now and began to speak. 'It's noth—'

'THE TREES HAVE EARS,' boomed a voice behind him.

'Ooh! Wha—? Oh, it's only you, Friar Donnan,' William heaved a sigh of relief.

Andrew, who had been stunned for a few moments, regained his composure. It was an old friar – a monk, a priest. In his hands he held the Holy Bible. Andrew sneezed again and gave a low, clearing cough.

'I'm sure, Father Donnan, if you'll excuse me, that is utter nonsense—'

'THE TREES HAVE EARS...' said Friar Donnan in his booming voice once again, then turned on his heels and vanished.

'What does he mean?' asked William, puzzled.

'Oh, he's a little crazy,' said Andrews, 'He's one of these monks who went all the way to China to learn something of medicine and wizardry. Ever since he came back, we've all felt he's a little off his rocker.'

William and Andrew walked on, once again discussing their strategy quietly. They hadn't gone very far when Andrew got a coughing fit. And again, the booming voice rang behind them : 'THE TREES HAVE EARS!'

It was Friar Donnan again! But before Andrew and William could ask him anymore, he vanished as mysteriously as he had appeared.

'What's wrong with him?' growled an angry Andrew, whose sore throat was already making him irritable.

'Maybe he's trying to warn us of something in this forest...' William whispered. 'Maybe ...the English are hidden right here, listening to every word that we're saying... waiting for the right moment to strike!'

'Or maybe he's just talking about these mushrooms – or plants – I don't know which,' Andrew said, pointing to the large, brown, fleshy fungi that grew abundantly

on the tree trunks. 'They look just like ears, don't they?' And to tell the truth, they remarkably did look like ears – gigantic human ones.

'Oh, that's the old tree-ear or wood-ear plant,' said William. 'What's there to talk about it? I think it's something else. I'm sure it's a warning!'

Andrew rubbished the notion and pushed William to move on. But every time he coughed a little loudly or cleared his throat, Friar Donnan appeared out of nowhere to announce that 'the trees had ears'.

***

William was worried now. He stopped discussing strategies with Andrew and looked around more carefully. He couldn't see anyone hiding in the bushes or behind the trees. But, perchance, his glance fell on the treetops! To his horror, he found English soldiers dressed in camouflage, lying in wait for the Scottish army!

Both the knights rushed back to King Bruce with the news. Their timely information gave the Scots an edge over the English, and they won the battle! After all the excitement was over, Friar Donnan was summoned to the king's court for a reward. After all, it had been his revelation that the English soldiers were lurking in the treetops, listening in to the knights' conversation!

'So, tell us, Friar Donnan,' began King Bruce, while the heroes of the battle, Andrew and William, looked on. 'How did you find this ingenious way of warning our troops? I am indeed pleased with your wit.'

Friar Donnan looked puzzled. 'I didn't warn anyone,' he said.

'But, but – you told William and Andrew—' it was the king's turn to look surprised. 'Then what were you saying about the trees having ears?'

'Oh, I wasn't talking about the war or soldiers at all,' said Friar Donnan cheerfully. 'I noticed that Lord Andrew was having quite a nasty bit of sore throat. The fungal mushrooms – what we call the tree-ear or wood-ear, is edible, and can be used as a cure for the ailment.'

It was now William's turn to look sheepish while Andrew looked smug. He had been right after all! But the battle had got them their freedom and Scotland had become an independent country.

Is there really a fungus that looks like human ears?

Yes, there is !

Jew's ear, wood-ear, jelly ear and tree-ear are the common names given to the fungus ***Auricularia auricula-judae,*** which is a species of edible fungus found worldwide. It has anti-tumour and cholesterol-lowering properties, and helps in the treatment of diabetes and blood clotting.

However, what makes it really stand out is its physical appearance: its close likeness to the structure of the human ear. It grows on the wood of hardwoods or conifers, generally during monsoons or when humidity and moisture are high. The fungus' shape ranges from disc-shaped to ear-shaped to irregular and floppy. It is brown to reddish brown, and the flesh is rubbery and gelatinous.

In the West, *A. auricula-judae* was used in folk medicine (even until the nineteenth century) for several health issues, such as sore throats, eye strain and jaundice. Although it is not widely consumed in the West, it has long been popular in China. In fact, to meet the demand for it, China imported large amounts of the fungus from Australia during the early twentieth century. Today, the fungus is a popular Chinese ingredient in food and medicine. It is also used as a blood tonic in Ghana.

21

SURVIVING WITHOUT WATER

'Enough, Velu,' scolded Mummy. 'Come out now, this very minute!'

Velu, the baby elephant, was in no mood to listen. He was still splashing around in the pond, drawing up water in his tiny trunk and squirting it all around. The rest of the elephants had already gone on ahead.

Velu's father gave him a stern look. 'You better come out this very minute, young man,' he said, 'or no sugarcane sticks for you!'

Velu's elder brother, Kuttan, merrily raised his trunk and stuck his tongue out at him, as if to say he would eat Velu's share of sugarcane as well. Velu was alarmed and pouted at Kuttan.

'Wait, I am coming,' he said hurriedly, as his family joined the herd and started walking away.

Velu was a spirited little elephant, the youngest in his herd. Everyone liked him because he was smart and intelligent, and endeared himself to anyone in no time. Living in the lush green land of Kerala, it was no surprise that he loved to frolic in the water. But Velu liked to be in the water *all* the time. He spent more time than anyone else in the pond and often wasted a lot of water just in play.

That morning, Velu had already spent two hours in the pond and wanted to stay on. But his father's warning made him look up and, half-heartedly, he got out of the water and solemnly joined his herd.

'You shouldn't even be allowed in the pond,' said his mother in an exasperated voice. 'Once you get in, you don't come out! The fish were complaining about you yesterday. They said they are worried that there wouldn't be a pond left for them!'

Velu giggled. 'Oh Ma, that can't be true,' he said. 'We have an entire herd, with the biggest elephants in the land. They have been using the pond for ages now, and the pond is still there! How can a baby elephant like me make so much of a difference?'

'The fact is that you do waste a lot of water,' said his father. 'When we have a resource, let's use it wisely. After all, we cannot live without water. No animal in this world can.'

'Well, then I shall become like your friend, the camel,' said Velu. 'I will start carrying water around in my hump.' And he did an imitation of Mr Camel lumbering along slowly. Kuttan giggled in delight and raised his trunk in approval.

'Stop being so mean, kids,' said their father disapprovingly. 'It's wrong to make fun of someone like that. Do you know how much he has to struggle and how many days he has to go without water in the desert? You boys aren't going to learn a lesson this way. I should ask him to give you both a lecture.'

'He just says that,' whispered Kuttan to Velu, reassuring him. 'I don't think he really means it.'

So a few days later, when Velu found Mr Camel at his home, he was quite surprised. But what puzzled him more was how Mr Camel had managed to come so quickly from the deserts of Saudi Arabia.

'Ah, there you are, Velu,' said the camel enthusiastically. '*Kefhaalek*? How are you?

'I am fine, Uncle, thank you,' said Velu, a little apprehensive about what was to come.

'Your father called me here so that I could give you a lecture,' he whispered and winked, as if it was a joke between them.

Velu sighed. He prepared himself for a long class on being a sensible elephant who would not waste water. Instead, the camel asked him, 'Would you like to come with me to Saudi Arabia?'

Velu stared at him open-mouthed. 'B-but how will we go?' stammered Velu.

The camel winked again. 'I have a secret.' Saying this, he drew out a big red carpet with pretty tassels at the corners. As soon as the camel spread it out, the carpet seemed to get a life of its own. It zoomed around them, and then floated down and hovered a foot above the ground near Velu. 'This will take us to Saudi Arabia in no time !'

Velu was awestruck. This had to be the magical flying carpet that he had heard about in the Arabian Nights stories!

'Come now, hop on!' cried the camel.

***

Velu jumped onto the carpet along with the camel, and it zoomed off into the skies. They landed in the deserts of Saudi Arabia soon enough. All around was a vast expanse of sand, with not a drop of water anywhere. The sun beat down on them hard, and soon enough, Velu was thirsty. But the camels were coolly walking around, not in the least bothered!

'Uncle, how do you manage to live here?' cried Velu in distress. 'There isn't any water around! Do your humps really store water?'

'Our humps store fat, not water,' said the camel. 'When we do get water, we drink as much as we can, and this excess water is stored in our blood.'

The camel then pointed to another animal, which looked very much like the cats back home, but was the colour of sand. 'See those sand cats? They're desert animals too, like us, and can go without water for a long period of time. But, eventually, we all need to drink water.'

Velu nodded in wonder. The camels hardly got water to drink, forget playing with it! The camel seemed to sense his thoughts and smiled. 'Let's go to Australia now,' he said. 'There's someone you should meet.'

They zoomed off to Australia on the magic carpet and landed in a forest. But, funnily, all the trees were the same – eucalyptus trees!

Velu spotted a small bear-like creature munching on some leaves. 'What animal is that?' he asked.

'That's the koala bear,' said the camel. 'He does not drink water by choice, because the eucalyptus leaves that he eats contain enough water to keep him from getting thirsty. So unless there is a really bad drought, he won't drink water at all.'

Velu wondered if he could eat the eucalyptus leaves too. He broke a few and began to munch on them, but he didn't like the taste much. He decided he wouldn't eat eucalyptus leaves unless all the water in Kerala got over!

They got on the carpet again. Velu thought they were going back to Kerala, but they landed elsewhere. 'We are in Death Valley, in California, United States,' the camel announced, 'And meet my friend, the kangaroo rat, who never drinks water ever.'

A small rodent emerged from a burrow. It had long, powerful hind legs on which it stood and hopped around, just like the kangaroo.

'Do you eat eucalyptus leaves too?' asked Velu.

'No, we eat seeds,' replied the kangaroo rat. 'But our bodies are designed to retain moisture in every possible way. Our kidneys make urine that is 17 times more concentrated than blood, by drawing back into the body as much excess water as it can.'

Velu realized how carefully other animals adjusted their needs to save water! He started thinking seriously about changing his ways. The camel saw Velu's thoughtful face and smiled. He didn't say anymore and took Velu back home after that. Nobody knew where he had been. But Velu had returned a wiser and more responsible elephant, who knew the value of water.

How important is water for animals?

Drinking water regularly is essential for most animals, though there are a few like camels and sand cats, which can go without water for long periods of time. They have evolved mechanisms to survive in desert conditions.

While the sand cat obtains water from its prey, the camel drinks between 20–100 gallons of water when it can, and this water is stored in its bloodstream. Its red blood cells, unlike that of humans and other mammals (which are circular) are oval.

When a camel drinks water, its red blood cells bloat to twice their size, but don't burst. Even in times of water scarcity, the oval shape of the cells prevents them from rupturing due to dehydration. The hump, meanwhile, comes in use when the camel faces starvation – the fat reserves are then broken down to provide nourishment.

The koala bears of Australia do not drink water by choice. They eat eucalyptus leaves, which contain a lot of water, thus fulfilling their need for moisture. Unless forced by a severe drought or a scarcity of eucalyptus plants, the koala will not drink water directly. The spinifex hopping mouse, found in Australia, also manages to survive without water in desert-like conditions.

The kangaroo rat of Death Valley (California, United States) does not drink a drop of water in its entire lifetime, which is about 10 years. It saves moisture in every way it can. It feeds on seeds, which it stores in its burrow, letting them absorb as much moisture as they can. The rat's kidneys are also efficient in super-concentrating urine, so that water loss is minimal. The kidney is made of units called nephrons that filter blood to make urine. The 'loop of Henle' – a part of the nephron that is involved in re-absorbing water – is longer in the nephrons of these kangaroo rats than that of other mammals, helping them to prevent water loss.

22

QUACK-QUACK! WHERE'S OUR MOTHER?

Napoleon, the sheepdog, was in a very, very bad mood. None of the other farm animals dared to cross his path that day, for they knew what a temper he had. He lay sulking in his kennel, while they whispered to each other.

'What's the matter with old Nappy?' asked the hen to the horse.

'Shhh!' said the horse. 'He better not catch you calling him that! He hates being called Nappy!' They both giggled. 'It's all because that silly red ball he plays with is missing since morning. You know he can't bear to part with it.'

'Well, where can it go?' said the hen. 'Must be somewhere around here on the farm!'

'I think the farmer took it into the house for his child to play with,' said the horse. 'Goodness knows where the kid must have dumped it!'

Just then, the duck passed that way, humming a happy tune, quite unmindful of the grave situation all around. Napoleon growled in annoyance. Here he was, worried to death about his missing red ball, and here was a silly bird crooning away a melody. Seeing Napoleon's fury, the hen hurriedly drew the duck to a corner, before the sheepdog could act any further.

'Hey, Ducky, watch it!' said the hen in a low voice. 'This is no time to sing!'

'Why ever not?' asked the duck, quite puzzled.

'Well, haven't you heard? Napoleon's favourite red ball is missing!'

'Ha! What a thing to worry about!' said the duck indignantly. 'I have better things to do, like keeping a few tasty snacks ready for my little babies when they hatch from my eggs.' She gave the hen a cold glance. 'Now, if you'll excuse me,' she said and began waddling towards the river.

'That was quite a snub,' remarked the horse, as the hen looked on stupefied.

'Well, she always had her nose in the air,' said the hen.

Just then, a loud commotion could be heard from the barn.

'Looks like duck's babies have hatched!' cried the hen. 'Let's go and have a look!'

It was quite a rush. Everyone, except the sheepdog, wanted to see the newborn ducklings. But when they all reached the place, they were stunned into silence. Only the quacks of the ducklings could be heard.

'Make way! Make way for the mother!' came a voice, as the duck jostled her way through the crowd of animals to reach her ducklings. 'Why, my babies', she started crooning. 'You've all arrived—' She stopped short, seeing all her six ducklings nestled up close to a bright red ball. Each of them turned lovingly to the ball and quacked 'Mama' by turns.

'Er...where were you, Duckie?' asked a goat. 'Looks like they think the ball is their mother.'

'I...I had gone down to the river...just a few moments ago...' stuttered the shocked Duckie. But she soon recovered. 'But this is nonsense! How can they think the ball is their mother? Wait till I get to them, they'll know I'm their mother'. She marched forward.

'Kids, look – it's me, your mother,' the mother duck announced proudly.

But the ducklings gave her a casual glance and turned back to the red ball. 'Mama,' said the ducklings to the ball.

'Look at me, I'm your real mother!' the duck said again. 'That's just a ball!'

The ducklings looked at her. Again, they shook their heads, turned to the ball, and quacked, 'Mama!'

All the animals tittered.

Amid all the commotion, Napoleon walked in, growling his way through. It looked like someone had sneaked to him about the whereabouts of his missing red ball. The moment he spotted it, Napoleon rushed towards it. He picked it up in his mouth, flicked away two ducklings that were hanging on to it and walked out with his head held high, while the ducklings cried in despair.

'Mama gone,' they quacked.

No amount of the mother duck's words, consolation or rebukes could make the ducklings see sense. 'We want Mama,' they said, as they walked out of the barn, trying to find where the red ball had gone. Napoleon, meanwhile, had hidden the ball deep inside his kennel and flopped down at the entrance to guard it.

The ducklings walked down in a single file, looking all around for their mother. 'Where's Mama?' they quacked from time to time. But they couldn't find the ball.

'They might get tired of it and accept the duck as their mom,' said a relieved hen.

But alas, that was not to happen! For a ripe, round orange fell down from the orange tree, right in the midst of the ducklings!

'Mama!' they cried joyfully, hugging the orange.

'What's the connection?' asked the confused horse.

'The ball is round, and so is the orange,' remarked the hen. 'Remove the orange now before they get attached to it.'

So the horse immediately picked up the orange and swallowed it.

The bewildered ducklings looked around for their 'mother' again. And that was when the animals heard the farmer starting his red tractor!

'MAMA! MAMA!' cried the excited ducklings, as they tore behind the red tractor, while the rest of the animals ran behind them to stop them. The farmer drove on, unaware of the retinue of ducklings, hens, goats and pigs following his tractor. At last, they managed to hold down the ducklings.

'What was the connection this time?' asked the horse, exasperated.

'The red colour, I suppose,' said the hen.

Mother Duck was crying her heart out. 'Oh, my poor babies', she wailed. 'They'll have to grow up without a real mother!'

Napoleon acted as though nothing had happened. 'There's no way I'm giving my ball away as a mother for some dippy ducklings', he muttered.

The hen thought for a while. 'Maybe you can still become their mother, Duckie,' she said, and ran to fetch a red rag cloth, which she fixed around the duck's body. The moment the ducklings saw the red cloth, they ran back to Mother Duck.

'Mama', they said happily, snuggling up to her at last!

How do birds like ducks identify their mother?

Scientists have found that when baby animals such as ducklings are born, they begin to identify and follow their mother around through a process called 'imprinting,' It is a natural biological phenomenon that allows many newborn mammals and birds to form a bond with their mother as well as provide them with information about their own identity. Though there is 'sensitive time period' for this to occur for birds like ducks, geese and turkeys that start walking as soon as they hatch, the imprint occurs instantly – often making ducklings assume any moving object – sometimes even inanimate objects – to be their mother.

This kind of behaviour suggests that ducks aren't very smart. But, on the contrary, scientists have proved that this very behaviour suggests remarkable ability for abstract thinking and logical reasoning – a quality of highly intelligent species. Ducks even outperform animal species that are considered 'smarter' in certain aspects of reasoning. Just hours after birth, they understand concepts like 'same' and 'different,' remember them and apply them to never-before-seen objects with no social cues or training. In an experiment, ducklings were found to follow objects similar in shape or colour to the objects shown to them immediately after they were hatched, thus proving their ability to match colours and shapes.

23

HOW ONE DISASTER DESTROYED ANOTHER

It was another dry, sunny morning of the year 1666, and London city was abuzz with activity. People were out on the streets, most of them heading to work; women chatted and gossiped with each other at the street corners, and children ran about.

It was quite another matter that conditions in the city were not as pleasant. Houses were built too close together for comfort or safety, using oak timber and painted with tar. The streets were dirty with sewage flowing right through the centre of the street, and garbage piled up in mounds all around. People walked with their noses covered with handkerchiefs, or buried in posies – bunches of sweet-smelling flowers.

Ten-year-old Ralph, however, sat morosely on the street with a tear-stained face. Adults refused to look his way, and children in the street, who had earlier been his friends, gave him helpless looks as they passed him. Ralph hardly noticed them, though. He seemed completely unaware of the overpowering stench that hung over London those days – of filth, disease and death.

On the other side of the street, Ralph could see Thomas Farriner, the king's baker, loading loaves of bread and biscuits on to a cart. It was meant for the Navy, and two soldiers were helping Farriner load the cart. Ralph was suddenly aware of his stomach rumbling. He realized he hadn't eaten anything properly for several days except for the few scraps of food that his neighbours had been kind enough to hand him.

He went up to where the baker stood shouting instructions to his helper and two apprentices. He didn't notice Ralph till he started speaking.

'Sir,' Ralph said, in a weak voice, 'It's been a week. Pop's in bed with the plague. Gimme a bit of loaf.'

Farriner ignored him at first and continued shouting at his servants. Ralph finally tugged at his apron, in a bid to attract his attention.

'Geroff, you!' snarled Farriner, and shoved Ralph to the ground. 'The loaves are fer the king, not fer the likes of you. Now, be off with you!'

The soldiers laughed. Ralph crawled away, sobbing. His father hadn't eaten anything either. He moved to a corner and watched them secure the cart and begin to ride away.

Ralph started running behind the cart as it made its way through the street. What if a loaf fell off? He would get something to fill his stomach and a little to sneak in to his father.

One of the soldiers saw him running after the cart. Taking pity on him, he took a broken bit of loaf and threw it towards him. ''Ere, take this!'

Ralph caught the bread just in time. His heart full of gratitude towards the soldier, Ralph ran back to his 'house'.

***

It had been a week since Ralph had started spending his days out on the street. Ever since his father had fallen sick, he had been forced to spend his days outside while his father lay in the tiny garret – a single-room attic at the top of a building – that had been their home. The neighbours had forced Ralph to stay away from his father, saying that he would go down with the plague too. They painted a huge red cross on the door of the garret, with the words 'Lord have mercy upon us!'

Ralph now rushed up the steps of the narrow, winding, rickety staircase to the garret. He hoped he wouldn't bump into anyone on the way. A few rats scurried across his path in the darkness as he reached the top landing. He slowly opened the door, hoping that the creaking hinges wouldn't alert the other tenants in the building. His father lay there in the single worn-out bed that they had. Red blisters on his skin, or 'buboes' as they were called, made him unsightly and repulsive. Ralph hardly cared, though. He ran inside, calling to his father. 'Pop, look what I got!'

Every time Ralph managed to sneak in, his father managed to lift his head and give him a weak smile, despite the fever and weakness. 'God made me sick today so that you can survive tomorrow,' he used to tell Ralph. But, today, he did not stir.

'Pop? Pop?' Ralph kept calling. But there was no answer. With a pang, Ralph realized that his father must have died, just like the thousands of the poor in London who had fallen prey to the same disease. He gave out a cry and rushed downstairs, tears running down his face. A few people in the lower floors heard his cries and came rushing out to enquire.

'There's a dead one on the first floor too,' said a man, once the matter was clear to all. 'The old lady is dead as well.'

'Throw away the bodies when they come to take away the dead,' said another. 'Here they come now!'

A cry rang through the streets. 'Bring out yer dead! Bring out yer dead!' The city of London had grown so accustomed to people dying of the plague that there was no more ceremony about disposing of the dead. People were ready to get rid of the plague-infected corpses as soon as they could, so they wouldn't risk getting the disease themselves. Every day, there came drivers of dead-carts, calling out to the townsfolk to bring out the bodies of the plague victims, so that they could be dumped all together into the huge pits dug to accommodate the large number of people who died.

Ralph watched helplessly as his father's body was loaded on one of the carts and taken away. He didn't know what to do anymore. He sat outside in the street, like a statue, knowing neither hunger nor pain.

***

Night fell, but Ralph couldn't sleep. He sat there in the street, his eyes wide open. A strong wind blew, giving him a slight shiver. He didn't know why he was waiting there, but he couldn't get himself to go back to the garret where he had found his father lying dead that morning.

He watched Thomas Farriner wind up his baking and shut down his bakery. Ralph saw the baker drawing the curtains of his windows, signalling his going upstairs to bed. Ralph absent-mindedly stared at the bakery as he considered his fate and the turn of events.

He saw a few sparks of light in the bakery through the curtained windows. The baker hadn't put his oven out, maybe, thought Ralph, and waited. He would come down and do it soon enough. It was past midnight, but it looked like the baker had not come down again. Ralph felt a strange foreboding as he saw an intense glow inside the bakery. The next thing he saw was the fancy curtains on fire!

'FIRE! HELP! THERE'S A FIRE!' cried Ralph at the top of his voice, but it didn't look like anybody was awake enough to hear him. The entire bakery was on fire now, with the flames licking the upper floor. Ralph went and pounded on the doors of all the houses on the street, shouting at the top of his voice. 'Help! The bakery's on fire!'

Soon people came tumbling out, armed with buckets of water. Try as they might, they could not put out the fire. As Ralph watched, the fire spread from house to house, street to street. The strong wind, the wooden houses and the tar coating only made matters worse. Now there were many more homeless people on the streets, along with Ralph. And with the people, came hundreds of rats! They rushed out of the sewers as the heat rose; yet most were killed in the fire. The fire fanned itself into an inferno and raged for four days, burning down half of London.

At the end of it all, Farriner, the careless baker, denied starting the fire. He alleged that it was a well-planned plot by foreigners to destroy London. But Ralph knew only too well what the truth was.

What good came of the Great Fire? The city of London was almost wiped out, but so were the rats. Miraculously, when the rats disappeared, so did the plague! The city was then rebuilt with better planning, so that its citizens could have a better place to live. And of course, our young hero, Ralph, got a chance to begin his life all over again!

Did the fire really wipe out the plague?

Yes, it did!

The Great Plague of 1665 and the Great Fire of 1666 were two huge disasters that hit London.

Bubonic plague was a disease carried by the fleas that lived on the bodies of rats. It is caused by a bacterium called *Yersinia pestis*, which can affect both humans and animals. However, rats seem to have an inborn immunity to the disease, and humans are the worst affected. Most of the transmission occurs between rodents and fleas. But when an infected flea bites a human, the disease is transmitted and can spread among humans through coughing and sneezing too.

These bacteria have the ability to suppress and avoid normal immune response systems such as phagocytosis (where our immune system 'eats up' the foreign bodies) and antibody production (our basic immune response against foreign bodies or 'antigens'). Symptoms include fever, chills, muscle aches, headache, sneezing and vomiting, red blisters on the skin and a swelling of the lymph nodes called 'buboes'.

The Great Plague of London was the last epidemic of the bubonic plague in England, and it was ended by the Great Fire that ravaged the city. When the fire broke out, it killed or drove out all the rats, which were the carriers of the plague.

24

THE VOLLEYBALL MATCH IN GIR FOREST

'Any luck yet?' called Dipu the langur from atop the tree.

'Nothing,' called back Jai, who was furiously searching in the shrubbery all around him.

'Well, get it back as soon as possible,' said Dipu, sounding annoyed. 'We have just a week left and there you go and lose the ball!'

'Well, I didn't lose it on purpose!' Jai flared up. 'You know, I just hit it a bit harder than usual.'

'Well, you'll be responsible for the team's loss of face when we don't have a ball next week,' said Dipu, equally annoyed. 'I'm going back to my tree,' he said, and went swinging away on the branches. 'And be careful about the lions!' he called out a warning.

Dipu and Jai were grey langurs, a type of monkey, and they lived in the Gir forest in Gujarat with their tribe. Unlike most monkeys who spent their time eating, grooming and fooling around, Jai and his friends were serious volleyball players. Exactly how they had learnt the game was a mystery, but the elders suspected that some of the younger langurs had stealthily gone visiting human homes and watched the game being played in a field and on the flat box called the television.

The ball they played with was one of the many items left behind by the absent-minded visitors at Gir Forest National Park. With some serious practice, they managed to become very good volleyball players. So confident were they that they challenged the Nilgiri langurs to a match. But during practice, Jai hit the ball so hard that it flew right out of view. Jai was worried. What if they didn't find the ball? How would they face the Nilgiri langurs next week? So now he was left on his own to find the ball.

The ball was nowhere to be seen. Jai could hear a lion's roar in the distance and began to panic. But he kept moving forward, hoping he would find the ball soon. He was now in lion territory, and he jumped at every small sound. Yet, he kept going and finally reached the edge of a lake. He peered out through the tall grass that bordered the edges, and to his horror, found his ball floating on the water – in the middle of the lake!

Jai sat down right there and cried. What would he tell his team now? He hated the water and knew he wouldn't be able to swim and get the ball back.

Dejected, he made his way back home. His team was waiting eagerly for him. The youngest of them came forward excitedly. 'Bro, where's the ball?' he asked. 'You said you would get it back!'

Jai sighed. 'It's gone now,' he said. 'Gone forever.'

'Why, what do you mean?' cried Dipu.

'It fell in the lake,' said Jai, and a collective gasp went around. 'But don't worry, I'll find a substitute for it soon.'

***

Jai left home the same evening, unable to bear Dipu's taunts and the dark looks his team gave him. He went around the big forest, hoping he would find some other ball left behind like the first one, but with no luck. After a long, hard search, Jai sat down to rest under a tree. Night had fallen. As he sat there, thinking what to do next, something came rolling by him.

Jai stared wide-eyed at this new object that was rolling around. It was the colour of the sand that covered the ground. It looked very much like a ball, but it seemed to be covered in overlapping scales. And, funnily, the ball had a tail!

The 'ball' rolled all around the langur for a while, and then came and lay motionless at his feet. Jai wondered if he could touch it. He bent down slowly and poked the ball with his finger. Suddenly, the ball unrolled itself and became an animal!

Jai was amazed. The 'ball' was no longer a spherical body. It had become a four-legged creature, with a

cone-shaped head, an elongated body and a long tail. It was covered in pinkish-brown scales. It grinned at Jai. 'Hi!' it said.

'What are you?' Jai asked, and then immediately realized his mistake, 'Uh, umm...sorry, I mean, who are you?'

The 'ball' giggled. 'My name is Gola,' it said. 'I'm a pangolin.'

Seeing Jai's blank face, it clarified – 'An anteater.'

Jai seemed to understand now. 'How come I've never seen you around here before?' he asked.

'Could be because I usually go out at night?' Gola replied. 'And there aren't many of us anyway.'

'You did give me a start!' complained Jai. 'How do you become a ball?'

'I can curl up into a ball whenever I like,' replied Gola. 'That's my defence against lions and tigers! They can't eat a scaly ball, can they? These scales are my armour.'

Jai marvelled at the pangolin's special ability. He had so far thought that monkeys had the most flexible bodies in the animal kingdom. But here was a creature that could effortlessly compress its long body into a sphere!

Jai and Gola became friends. They started walking through the forest together.

'So why were you crying?' asked Gola, stopping now and then to eat insects.

'We have a volleyball match coming up, and I lost our ball,' said Jai sadly. 'That was the only ball we had. If I don't find one soon, the Nilgiri langurs are going to laugh at us.'

The pangolin stopped at an ant-hill again and slurped up a mouthful of ants. 'I've heard that the area you langurs live in is full of tasty insects,' he said. 'Is it true?'

'Well, definitely there are lots of insects there,' said Jai, who had never really tried eating the insects to find out how they tasted.

'If I become the ball for your match, will you let me eat the insects at your place?' asked Gola.

Jai couldn't believe his ears.

'Whaa-at?' he asked, confused.

'If I roll myself up and become a substitute ball for your volleyball match, can I eat my fill of insects there?' Gola repeated.

Jai was overcome with joy. 'Of course you can!' he said. 'Thank you, thank you, thank you so much for saying you'll be our ball!' He started to give a loud cheer but stopped short. 'Say, won't you be hurt with all that swinging around?'

'Not to worry,' said Gola confidently. 'My scales are made up of hard keratin, among the toughest materials known in Nature. I'll be absolutely fine!'

The next week, a spectacular volleyball match took place between the grey langurs of Gir Forest and the visiting Nilgiri langurs. And there's no doubt who won – Jai and Dipu carried away the Exotic Mixed Fruit Trophy, while the pangolin contentedly munched away at his reward of yummy (he thought!) insects. Meanwhile, the Nilgiri langurs decided they would not accept any more volleyball challenges from the grey langurs their whole lives!

Can the pangolin roll up into a ball?

Yes, it can!

Pangolins are found in many places in the world, including China and Africa. The Indian pangolin, or the scaly anteater, is found in India, Sri Lanka, Bhutan and Nepal. Pangolins are nocturnal animals that feed on insects. They have long, sticky tongues, which they use to draw out insects from narrow crevices. They have powerful limbs, but no teeth.

The fascinating thing about pangolins is that they have large, overlapping scales on their body, which act as a protective covering. These scales are made up of 'keratin' – the same protein that makes up human hair and nails. When attacked or threatened, the pangolin rolls itself up into a ball, with its face tucked under its tail.

How does it do that? This is possible because of the unique arrangement of its scales and the structure of the keratinized cells in the outer and inner layers. The scales are arranged in an overlapping pattern, with each scale surrounded by six other scales in a hexagonal manner. Each scale has three scales above, partially covering it, and three below, which it partially covers. While the outer layer of these scales, called the 'cuticle', has several layers of loosely attached keratinized cells, the interior structure has densely packed layers of keratinized cells called 'lamellae', which have an interlocking mechanism between them, leading to more flexibility, elasticity and bonding strength.

Some species of pangolins also secrete a strong, foul-smelling liquid from their anal glands as a form of defence. The pangolin is now an endangered species around the world as it is hunted for its meat and also for its body parts that are used in traditional medicine.

25

THE BEST ACTOR AWARD

'And the award for the best female actor goes to...Bessy Killdeer!' The garden erupted in applause as Bessy, the killdeer bird, proudly glided onto the stage to take the award. Clearing her throat, she started, 'I am honoured to receive the Bird's Oscar for Best Female Actor. I take this opportunity to thank my numerous fans, my biggest fans, all my fans who have been writing to me—'

'MUMMY! HELP!' came an urgent scream and Bessy shook herself awake. Blow! It had just been a dream, as usual. She sighed.

Bessy was a killdeer bird – a very common bird in North America – the home of Hollywood, where the most talented actors become famous in the whole wide world, admired by millions and millions. The birds of the continent had not escaped the Hollywood craze, and had their own movies and awards. And Bessy's one mission in life was to win the Birds' Oscar. She always wondered when she would become a star.

Her thoughts were interrupted once again by the persistent screams from her baby. 'Mummy! Help me catch this worm!' She flew over to find her chick struggling with a worm that was twice as long as himself, and she wrested it out of his beak.

'Don't try to get at things that aren't within your grasp!' she chided him and led him back to the safety of their nest under the bush. Her other three chicks were walking around clumsily, pecking at the ground. She couldn't daydream anymore until her husband came back home; she had to look after her chicks. She scolded herself mentally. How could she, a mother of four baby birds, dream of becoming an actor? 'I have to stop thinking of my stupid ambition,' she muttered to herself, and continued keeping a watch out for anything that spelt danger.

A long time passed, and Bessy was bored and annoyed. Why wasn't her husband back yet? She glanced around, and that was when she saw a keen pair of green eyes observing her baby birds. It was a cat, waiting to pounce on her little ones! Bessy was filled with horror. She called out to her kids in a high voice to come back to the nest. 'Killdeee! Killdeeeeee!'

Her babies knew what her call meant. They came running back to safety. The cat saw them move out of its reach and then spotted Bessy. The mother bird was a daydreamer, but she was a mom too! She ruffled up her feathers and spread out her tail and wings, to make herself appear bigger. 'Go away, Cat!' she said. 'Shoo! Don't you dare come near my little ones!' The cat seemed a little taken aback and pulled back a little. But he didn't take its eyes off Bessy and her little nest, where the babies were crouching under the bush.

Bessy knew that the cat wouldn't go away that easily. How could she save her little ones who couldn't even fly yet? She could only do one thing now: use herself as the bait!

She slowly moved away from her nest, hopping a little haphazardly, drawing the cat's attention. She kept walking away from her nest, hoping that the cat would come after her instead of her babies. 'Yoohoo, Mr Cat!' she called out. 'Care to catch me for dinner?'

The cat was amazed. What was wrong with this bird? Birds flew away when attacked. They didn't hop around on the ground like this one, inviting the enemy to attack! But the cat was hungry, and all he wanted was some food. The mother bird seemed a lot bigger than the babies, who seemed to have disappeared under the bush. Why waste a free lunch that was inviting him over? The cat blindly went after Bessy, forgetting all about the babies.

Bessy went on ahead, leading the cat to a nice little dance. She went this way and that, pretending that she couldn't fly. She spread out her wing in an awkward manner, as if it was broken. The cat was now convinced that Bessy was wounded and couldn't fly at all, and he could catch her easily.

The cat went after her cautiously, trying to get closer. Bessy, meanwhile, was putting on her act of being helpless – and enjoying herself thoroughly. She was having the time of her life, fooling the cat with her acting skills.

The duo was now far away from the nest, and Bessy waited a moment longer, to let the cat close enough to catch her. Just before he could clamp his paws on her, Bessy flew out of its reach!

'Ha-ha-ha! Fooled you, Mr Cat!' she called from above.

The cat was furious. 'I'll be back for you one day, you cunning bird!' he mewled, and bounded away angrily. Bessy flew back to her nest, relieved that her babies were safe for the time being. She found her husband back home.

'Where did you go leaving our babies alone?' he said worriedly. 'What if something had happened to them?'

Bessy didn't bother to explain – he had missed out on all the drama anyway.

'Why are you so late?' she asked.

'Because I went to get these – tickets for the Birds' Oscar Night tomorrow!' he said gleefully. Bessy was delighted, but also felt somewhat subdued when she remembered her dream. But they all went for the award ceremony the next day.

The Oscar night was a huge success, as awards were given away to the stars of the evening. Then

came the moment to present the Best Female Actor award. Bessy was only half listening. The eagle, who was the host, started speaking. 'Every year, we give away awards to the birds who have used their acting talent in movies to entertain all of us,' he said, 'but this time, we will be giving our Best Female Actor award to a mother bird, who, through her acting skills, managed to save the lives of her children. And the award goes to...Bessy Killdeer !'

Bessy couldn't believe her ears.

'Hurray for Mummy!' cried her children.

The eagle went on to describe how, he had observed Bessy lead a cat away from her nest by pretending to be injured. The entire gathering gave Bessy a standing ovation as she went on the stage to take her award. Bessy couldn't speak, though she had dreamt of that beautiful moment many, many times. But her heart was full of happiness as she stood there – the award within her grasp, and her dream fulfilled.

Can killdeer birds really act?

Yes, they can!

Killdeer birds are commonly found in North America. They have brown backs and wings, and a white breast with two black bands. They usually build their nests close to human settlements, and often under bushes or on gravel. Their eggs resemble the pebbles in the gravel and mostly go unnoticed, thus keeping them safe. The mother and father birds take turns to guard their eggs and young ones. If their eggs or chicks are threatened by a predator, the male or female bird performs its 'broken wing display' act, where it pretends to be injured and lures its enemy far away from the nest. The predator goes after the bird, hoping to catch the injured bird easily. However, the killdeer bird escapes before it can be caught!

ACKNOWLEDGEMENTS

From the time that I can remember, all that I've ever asked for are books. Reading got me under the skin and into the heads of a million fictional characters, and made my childhood magical, letting me dream a billion dreams and think a trillion thoughts.

Then it was no longer enough that I read stories. I wanted to write them too. Yet, it seemed like one of those things that as a child, you think you're perfectly capable of doing – and then you grow up and look down on the whole thing as a silly fantasy that sounds rather impossible. I'm surprised that despite all my misgivings and self-doubt, I held on to this far-fetched fantasy, and my books are finally seeing the light of day.

I think of all the kids who grew up to be 'successful' by adult standards but couldn't realize their childhood dreams; then I realize this is a miracle and a blessing, and that I have a lot to thank the Almighty for.

If God pulled me through to this end, there was my loving family pushing me towards it – my name as author on the book's cover is a result of a mother's penance. My mother, Shirley, made her whole life about me, so that I could achieve whatever I had set out to. My books are a testimony to her love and sacrifice, and she has always been that voice of strength and reassurance that got me through all my trials and challenges. My aunt, Asha, is the bibliophile who helped me follow in her footsteps, whose stories I looked forward to everyday from the time I was a child. Apart from my mother, she was the first one to read my stories and poetry, and inspire in me the confidence that I could, indeed, write.

My grandmother, Grace, who is a paradoxical treasure trove of affection, tradition, sarcastic wit and an attitude of glorious indifference to naysayers, is the reason I don't stop dreaming of more books to write and more challenges to take on. My uncle Santhosh and aunt Jolly are my silent pillars, whom I trust to speak up for me anytime I need them to.

I wonder what my grandfather, K.J. Joseph, who taught me to write, would be thinking now as he looks down upon me from heaven – I do hope I've done him proud.

It is difficult to find method in my madness, but two people whom I am proud to call all my own uncomplainingly stand by me and I'm glad to say they love me despite the various (sometimes unreasonable) goals I chase – my husband Vineeth (who has accepted most things about me wholeheartedly, and some, with resignation) and my son Vihann (who is too small to protest at the moment).

To all the above, I am ever grateful – for all they have done for me, and continue to do for me.

I thank my editor, Vatsala Kaul Banerjee, for believing in my stories, and working day and night to make *From Sea to Sky* and *From Root to Rain* perfect in every aspect. Dear Vatsala – it was your decision to read my submission that brought me this far, and I am ever grateful for everything you've done for me. I have learnt a lot from you, and I hope it reflects in all my future writing.

I thank my publishers, Hachette India, for seeing the potential in my stories and taking them to children all over the world. I thank Ishan Trivedi for the beautiful illustrations in the book that have brought my stories to life, and Sharanya Kunnath for the awesome cover design.

I also thank Usha Akella, well-known poet, who transformed my poetry through her crisp editing, giving me valuable lessons on how to improve my craft. Thank you, Usha!

I thank the *Hans India* newspaper, which carried my stories first as 'Nature Narratives' and gave me my first break as a regular columnist on the 'Young Hans' page. I thank Prof. K. Nageshwar, who was the then editor of the newspaper, for the opportunity, and Mr Ramu Sharma, the current editor, for granting me permission to compile my published stories as books.

I am grateful to the management and my colleagues at ICAR-CRIDA, Hyderabad, for all their support.

I remember all my friends from school to university, who read my stories, marvelled at them and assured me that one day I would be a proper author who would make them proud – thank you!

I thank all my teachers and professors, especially Ms Anita Naidu (Rosary Convent High School), Prof. K. Stevenson, Prof. K. Narender, Prof. Y.L. Srinivas and Prof. G.K. Subbarayudu (Osmania University) who always believed in me and encouraged me.

I thank all those – known and unknown – who have wished me well and played a role in bringing me to where I am today.

I thank all the children who will read my stories, and grow to love science and Nature through them. I hope that I can arouse in them the same magic that I felt as a child, and that they will be the reason that I write more stories, and more books.

After all, books are all that I've ever wanted. To read. And to write.

IMAGE COPYRIGHT INFORMATION

Liked *From Sea to Sky*? Then you'll love this book too!

FROM ROOT TO RAIN

Hidden Stories of Nature's Science

by Sneha Verghese

***

Plants that look like stones.
The cell and its self-destructing zones.
Seeds that catch on like claws.
Clocks in our bodies that tick without pause.
Dung beetles that are very choosy about...poop.
Bacteria with team spirit, working in a group.
Birds that behave like bats.
ARE THESE REALLY FACTS?

Find out about all these and more in this thrilling collection of 25 captivating stories that takes you up into the sky, under the sea, over hills, through jungles and across the world in a way you never thought possible.

Introducing keen young readers to fascinating science in the environment around them, these tales simplify complex concepts into easy-to-follow ideas, while answering questions, explaining scientific phenomena and sparking curiosity to explore the secret world of Nature.

Gear up for an exhilarating adventure of discovery!